Academic Writing Skills

Teacher's Manual 2

Peter Chin   Joseph Garner   Miklos Juhasz

Samuel Reid   Sean Wray   Yoko Yamazaki

79 Anson Road, #06-04/06, Singapore 079906

Cambridge University Press is part of the University of Cambridge.

It furthers the University's mission by disseminating knowledge in the pursuit of education, learning and research at the highest international levels of excellence.

www.cambridge.org

First published 2012
Reprinted 2018

Printed in Italy by Rotolito S.p.A.

ISBN 978-1-107-68236-8 paperback Teacher's Manual 2
ISBN 978-1-107-62109-1 paperback Student's Book 2

Cambridge University Press has no responsibility for the persistence or accuracy of URLs for external or third-party internet websites referred to in this publication, and does not guarantee that any content on such websites is, or will remain, accurate or appropriate.

Contributors: Peter Chin, Joseph Garner, Miklos Juhasz, Samuel Reid, Sean Wray, Yoko Yamazaki
Editor: Sean Wray

Academic Writing Skills has been developed by the Research and Development team at Waseda University International Co., Ltd., Tokyo.

Contents

Introduction to the Teacher's Manual

Academic Writing Skills is a three-level series which introduces the essential skills and strategies required to compose academic essays. *Academic Writing Skills 2* is the second book in the series. It contains four units, with each divided into parts (11 parts total in the book). An appendix of writing points is attached at the end of the book.

The *Academic Writing Skills 2 Teacher's Manual* has two parts:

Part 1: Lesson plans for each part of each unit (11 lesson plans total)

Part 2: The answer key to the exercises

General tips on using the textbook in class

For teachers and students, the textbook is designed to be followed directly. Therefore, each part of each unit has the following features:

1. **The goals of the lesson,** listed in bullet points at the beginning.
2. **Sections introducing teaching points** which describe a particular aspect of academic writing.
3. **Examples and exercises** to help deepen students' understanding of the teaching points.
4. **Review questions,** listed at the end to review the teaching points.

To best utilize the book's features and class time, it is suggested that teachers:

1. **State lesson goals.**
   Lesson goals are listed at the beginning of each part in the textbook. State these goals and/or write them on the board at the beginning of the lesson so students are focused on what they should be learning.
2. **Avoid lengthy explanations**.
   - Elicit key words and concepts from students whenever possible. Students may have read the points (if assigned as homework) or may already have some knowledge of these points.
   - Use concept check questions to make sure students understand both the components of an essay and their purpose.
3. **Have students work in pairs or groups.**
   Students can support each other's learning by doing the exercises or checking their answers collaboratively. A suggested size for small groups is 3 or 4 students.
4. **Review the lesson points.**
   Use the Review Questions (listed at the end of each part) at the end of the class or at the beginning of the next class to check students' understanding.

Assigning homework

1. **Reading** Reading of particular teaching points from the textbook can be assigned as homework. This will help when teaching these points in class, as students when elicited will be better able to answer questions on the points.

2. **Writing** The textbook presents individual aspects of essay writing, but does not contain a specific essay writing task. It is recommended that an essay writing task be assigned to supplement the lessons. Students can apply what they learn in each lesson to this writing task so that by a certain point in the course, they will have a completed academic essay.

- *The internet and its effect on education in your home country*
- *Is foreign language education in kindergarten too early for children?*
- *Gender equality rankings are consistently high in Scandinavian countries. Explain some of the major reasons for this.*
- *Some say developed countries should increase financial aid to poor countries. Others say developed countries should reduce such aid. Argue for one of the sides on this issue.*

Lesson plans

How to use the lesson plans

The lesson plans in this teacher's manual supplement the textbook by offering suggestions for:

- presenting the teaching points (the explanation under each section heading)
- conducting the practice exercises

There are a number of suggestions for each section. However, these suggestions are not meant to be followed in order. Rather, they should be viewed as a menu to choose from. Teachers should feel free to use some, all, or none of these ideas, or alternatively to supplement the textbook with their own ideas.

Text in the lesson plans that appears in *italics* denotes a suggested question or useful information to ask or share with students. Answers to the suggested questions appear in **bold** and follow (Answer) or (Possible answer).

UNIT 1

Part 1
Essay structure and the introductory paragraph

Essay structure

This section introduces a lot of information. However, it is important to note that all of the information will be covered in more depth later in the unit.

1. Introduce the idea of an essay by having students discuss these questions with a partner:
   - *What types of essays have you written in the past?*
   - *How long were they?*
   - *What topics did you write about?*

2. Explain:
   - *The first type of essay the textbook will cover is an expository essay – an essay that explains something.*

3. To elicit how much students know about essay organization:
   - Draw the following table on the board.

1	
2	
3	
4	
5	

   - Explain: *This is a five-paragraph essay. Each line represents a paragraph.*
   - Then elicit: *What is the type of paragraph that should go on each line?*
   - As students give correct answers, write them in the table.

   (Answer)

1	**Introduction**
2	**Body**
3	**Body**
4	**Body**
5	**Conclusion**

4. Emphasize:
   - *This textbook will focus on five-paragraph essays; however, the structure can be adapted for longer or shorter essays.*

Introductory, body, and concluding paragraphs
Option 1

1. Have students read the explanations in the textbook.

2. With books closed, elicit:
   - *What should an introductory paragraph contain?* (Answer: **Hook, building sentences, thesis statement**)

- *What should a body paragraph contain?* (Answer: **Topic sentence, supporting sentences, concluding sentence**)
- *What should a concluding paragraph contain?* (Answer: **Restated thesis, summary of main ideas, final thought**)

Option 2

1. Divide the class into groups of three.

2. Instruct one student in each group to read each section (i.e., one student reads about introductory paragraphs, one student reads about body paragraphs, and one student reads about concluding paragraphs).

3. Have students close their textbooks and summarize the information to each other.

4. Check understanding by asking:
   - *What should an introductory paragraph contain?* (Answer: **Hook, building sentences, thesis statement**)
   - *What is the purpose of an introductory paragraph?* (Answer: **To create interest in the topic, outline the writer's main ideas, and suggest how they will be presented**)
   - *What should a body paragraph contain?* (Answer: **Topic sentence, supporting sentences, concluding sentence**)
   - *What is the purpose of body paragraphs?* (Answer: **To explain in detail the main ideas presented in the thesis statement**)
   - *What should a concluding paragraph contain?* (Answer: **Restated thesis, summary of main ideas, final thought**)
   - *What is the purpose of a concluding paragraph?* (Answer: **To review the main ideas from the body paragraphs and leave the reader with a final thought**)

Five-paragraph essay structure

1. Have students look at the essay structure diagram on page 4 for one minute.

2. Have students close their books. Then ask them to draw the diagram on a blank piece of paper.

3. Ask students to compare their diagram with the one in the textbook.

4. Emphasize:
   - *The thesis statement is the most important sentence in the essay.*
   - *Each body paragraph must link to the thesis statement.*
   - *The thesis statement should be restated in the concluding paragraph.*

Exercise 1

Option 1

1. Have students work individually to:
   - skim the model essay.
   - identify the elements in the model essay (by writing the name of the element in the margin next to the appropriate section).
2. When done, have students compare answers with a partner.
3. Elicit answers.

Option 2

1. Divide the class into small groups.
2. Have students work collaboratively to:
   - skim the model essay.
   - identify the elements in the model essay (by writing the name of the element in the margin next to the appropriate section).
3. Elicit answers.

Option 3

1. Follow Option 1 or 2 above.
2. Then, in small groups, have students discuss this question: *How is solar power being used in your home country?*
3. Elicit answers.

Section 2 — The introductory paragraph

Option 1

1. Have students read the explanation.
2. With books closed, elicit:
   - *What is the purpose of an introductory paragraph?* (Answer: **To tell the reader the essay's topic, purpose, and main ideas**)
   - *What are the three elements of an introductory paragraph?* (Answer: **Hook, building sentences, thesis statement**)
3. Write the answers on the board.

Option 2

1. In small groups, have students discuss the answers to the following questions:
   - *What is the purpose of an introductory paragraph?*
   - *What are the three elements of an introductory paragraph?*
2. Have students use their textbooks to check their answers.

1. Writing a thesis statement

Option 1

1. Have students read the explanation.
2. With books closed, elicit:
   - *What should a thesis statement contain?* (Answer: **Topic of the essay, writer's position/ opinion/approach to the topic, the main ideas that will be used to support the writer's position**)
   - *Where is a thesis statement usually located?* (Answer: **At the end of the introductory paragraph**)
   - *How long is a thesis statement?* (Answer: **Usually one sentence in shorter essays**)
3. Emphasize:
   - *The thesis statement is the most important sentence in the essay as it is the answer to the essay question, which the rest of the essay will support.*

Option 2

1. Follow Option 1 above.
2. Elicit from students:
   - *What will the first body paragraph be about?* (Answer: **"providing efficient light safely"**)
   - *What will the second body paragraph be about?* (Answer: **"linking them to the global mobile community"**)
   - *What will the third body paragraph be about?* (Answer: **"increasing their independence"**)
3. Emphasize:
   - *The thesis statement provides a map to the essay.*

Option 3

1. Follow Option 1 above.
2. Write this question on the board: *How has the advent of online shopping affected the way retailers conduct business?*
3. Have students discuss the question in small groups.
4. Elicit ideas. (Possible answers: **Can sell to wider area, can collect customer data easily, need fewer staff**)
5. Use the ideas to write an answer to the question on the board. (Possible answer: **Online shopping has had a significant impact on retailers as it allows them to sell their products in a wider range of locations, easily collect customer data, and reduce staffing levels.**)
6. Explain that this answer is a thesis statement. It contains a topic (online shopping), a position (has had a significant impact on retailers), and main ideas (reduce staffing levels, easily collect customer data, and sell their products to a wider range of locations).

Exercise 2

Option 1

1. Have students complete the exercise individually.
2. Have students compare answers with a partner.
3. Elicit answers.

Option 2

1. Divide the class into pairs.
2. Have students work collaboratively to complete the exercise.
3. Elicit answers.

Option 3

1. Follow Option 1 or 2.
2. Then individually or in pairs, have students try to improve the thesis statements marked with an *X* by adding the missing elements.
3. Elicit answers.

2. Writing a "hook"

Option 1

1. Have students read the explanation.
2. With books closed, elicit:
   - *What is the purpose of a hook?*
   - *What are some common types of hooks?*

Option 2

1. Read, or write on the board, the following "hooks" one at a time:
   - *Many scientists believe that in the future, the average lifespan may be 150 years, 200 years, or even longer.*
   - *Some of the world's most successful entrepreneurs never graduated from college.*
   - *Statistics show that more people are killed in the United States by vending machines falling on them than by shark attacks.*
2. Elicit after each hook:
   - *Did I get your attention?*
   - *Why?*
3. Emphasize:
   - *A hook is meant to create interest in your essay.*

Exercise 3

Option 1

1. Have students complete the exercise individually.
2. Have students compare answers with a partner.
3. Elicit answers.

Option 2

1. Divide the class into pairs.
2. Have students work collaboratively to complete the exercise.
3. Elicit answers.

Option 3

1. Follow Option 1 or 2 above.
2. Have students look back at the model essay (page 5) and identify the type of hook that is used. (Answer: **A quotation**)

Exercise 4

Option 1

1. Explain:
   - *A hook must introduce the topic of the essay, and it must link to the sentence that follows.*
2. Have students complete the exercise individually.

3. Then have students compare answers with a partner.
4. Elicit:
   - *Which words link the appropriate hooks to the thesis?* (Answers: **c** – "modern life" and "enduring crowded streets, noise, endless advertisements, work, and stress"; **e** – "modern life" and "busier and busier")
   - *What is wrong with the incorrect answers?* (See answer key.)

Option 2

1. Follow Option 1 above.
2. Have students write an alternative hook for the essay.
3. Then have students:
   - swap their hooks with a partner.
   - give feedback on how effective their partner's hook is.

Option 3

1. Follow Option 1 or 2 above.
2. Have students underline the topic, position, and main ideas in the thesis statement. (Answer: **"The slow life movement [topic] has successfully led to [position] more and more people eating healthier food, a preference for locally produced over imported food, and an increase in the demand for organic and naturally grown crops." [main ideas]**)
3. Elicit:
   - *What will the first body paragraph be about?* (Answer: **"more and more people eating healthier food"**)
4. Re-emphasize:
   - *The thesis statement is a map of the essay.*

3. Writing building sentences

Option 1

1. Have students read the explanation individually. Then, in pairs and with books closed, have students summarize to each other what they read.
2. Check students' understanding of the key points by asking:
   - *What different kinds of information about the topic could be included in the building sentences?* (Answer: **History, relevant statistics, the current situation regarding the topic, attitudes towards the topic**)
   - *What are the different ways of organizing building sentences?* (Answer: **General to specific, familiar information to new information, chronologically**)

Option 2

1. Draw the following table on the board:

Hook
Thesis statement

2. Elicit from students:
   - *What is missing?* (Answer: **Building sentences**)

3. Have students discuss the following question in small groups:
   - *What types information can the writer give the reader in the building sentences in order to help the reader understand the essay?* (Answer: **History, relevant statistics, the current situation regarding the topic, attitudes towards the topic**)

4. Emphasize:
   - *This information can be organized from general to specific, from familiar information to new information, or chronologically.*
   - *Without effective building sentences, a reader will not be able to have a good understanding of the essay.*

Option 3

1. Have students look at the introductory paragraph of the model essay on page 10.

2. Then have students discuss:
   - *What kind of background information do the building sentences in this model essay provide?*

3. Elicit answers. (Answer: **They give some background on the history and current situation of the topic.**)

Exercise 5

Option 1

1. Have students work individually to put the building sentences in the correct order.

2. Then have students compare their answers in pairs or small groups.

3. Elicit answers.

Option 2

1. Follow Option 1 above.

2. Once the correct order has been reached, have students discuss this question: *How were the building sentences organized?*

3. Elicit answers. (Answer: **1. From general to specific. 2. Chronologically**)

Exercise 6

Option 1

1. As a class, brainstorm the topic "The threat of nuclear weapons." Note ideas on the board.

2. Have students read the hook and the thesis statement. Decide which of the ideas on the board are relevant.

3. Use these ideas to write the building sentences.

4. Have students discuss:
   - *How were the building sentences organized?* (Possible answers: **From general to specific; familiar information to new information, chronologically**)

5. Repeat the process for item 2 OR have students do it individually or in pairs.

6. Have students compare answers with another student or pair.

7. Elicit answers and write them on the board.

Option 2

1. Divide the class into small groups.

2. Have each group look at the topic for item 1. Have them discuss and note down what they know about "The threat of nuclear weapons."

3. Have students read the hook and thesis statement for item 1. Then have students work collaboratively to write building sentences. Have students assign one writer. Other students are to help the writer with:
   - vocabulary
   - grammar
   - organizing the sentences

4. Have students swap their building sentences with another group and discuss:
   - *How were the building sentences organized?* (Possible answers: **From general to specific; familiar information to new information, chronologically**)

5. Repeat step 2–4 for item 2.

UNIT 1

Part 2
Body paragraphs, concluding paragraphs, and outlining

| Section 1 | The body paragraph |

Option 1

Explain:

1. *In a five-paragraph essay, there should be three body paragraphs.*

2. *The body paragraphs provide evidence that supports the writer's position.*

3. *Each body paragraph should focus on one main idea from the thesis statement.*

4. *Each body paragraph needs a topic sentence, supporting sentences, and a concluding sentence.*

Option 2

1. Have students read the explanation.

2. With books closed, have students discuss:
   - *How many body paragraphs does a five-paragraph essay need?* (Answer: **3**)
   - *What is the purpose of the body paragraphs?* (Answer: **To provide evidence that supports the writer's position**)
   - *How many ideas should each body paragraph focus on?* (Answer: **1**)
   - *What are the three elements of a body paragraph?* (Answer: **A topic sentence, supporting sentences, and a concluding sentence**)

1. Writing a topic sentence

Option 1

1. Explain:
   - *The first sentence of each body paragraph is the topic sentence.*
   - *The topic sentence needs a topic and a controlling idea.*
   - *The controlling idea is what the writer wants to say about the topic.*

2. Have students read the explanation.

3. Then have students look at the second and third body paragraphs in the model essay (page 6) and circle the topic and underline the controlling idea for each.

4. Have students compare answers in pairs.

5. Elicit answers.
   (Answer)
   - **Body paragraph 2: topic = "the power of these solar panels"; controlling idea = "is also being used to help people in developing countries connect to global communication networks"**
   - **Body paragraph 3: topic = "solar power"; controlling idea = "people in developing countries are able to live their lives with greater autonomy"**

6. Emphasize:
   - *All of the following sentences in the paragraph must support this controlling idea.*
   - *After reading a topic sentence, the reader should be able to predict what the paragraph will be about.*

Option 2

1. Write the following on the board: *The internet has changed the world.*

2. Elicit:
   - *If this were a body paragraph's topic sentence, could you predict what the paragraph would be about?* (Answer: **No; it is too broad. You could tell that the paragraph is about the internet, but it is impossible to know what the specific focus is.**)

3. In pairs or small groups, have students brainstorm:
   - *How has the internet changed the world?*

4. Elicit answers and write them on the board. (Possible answers: **It has made it easier to access information; it has made it easier to communicate across large distance**s)

5. Add one of the reasons to the original sentence on the board (e.g.: *The internet has changed the world in that it has made it easier to access information.*)

6. Explain:
   - *The topic sentence is now effective because it has both the topic and a controlling idea.*
     (Underline the topic and controlling idea: **The internet has changed the world** [topic] **in that it has made it easier to access information.** [controlling idea])
   - *As result, the reader can now predict what the paragraph will be about.*

7. Have students read the explanation on pages 13 and 14.

8. Emphasize:
   - *All of the following sentences in the paragraph must support this controlling idea.*

| Exercise 1 |

Option 1

1. Have students answer the questions individually.

2. Then have students compare answers with a partner.

3. Elicit answers.

Option 2

1. Divide the class into pairs.

2. Have students work collaboratively to complete the exercise.

3. Elicit answers.

Option 3

1. Follow Option 1 or 2 above.

2. Then, individually or in pairs, have students try to improve the topic sentences marked with an *X*.

3. Elicit answers.

2. Organizing supporting sentences

Option 1

1. Have students read the explanation.

2. Then, in pairs and with books closed, have students summarize to each other what they read.

3. Elicit:
   - *What is the purpose of the supporting sentences?* (Answer: **To show why the controlling idea is true**)
   - *What are the three different types of supporting sentences?* (Answer: **State a reason, provide an example, and provide an explanation**)
   - *How many times may the "waltz" pattern be repeated in one paragraph?* (Answer: **3**)

Option 2

1. Follow Option 1 above.

2. Then draw the following table on the board:

1	Topic sentence
2	
3	
4	
5	
6	
7	
8	Concluding sentence

3. Elicit:
   - *Based on the example paragraph on page 15, what are the missing types of sentences?* (Answer: **2. Reason; 3. Evidence; 4. Explanation; 5. Reason; 6. Evidence; 7. Explanation**)

4. Emphasize:
   - *Every sentence must relate to the controlling idea.*
   - *If a sentence/point is not relevant, it should not be included.*
   - *The relevance of every piece of evidence must be explained.*

Option 3

To focus on transitional expressions:

1. Have students look at the model paragraph on page 15.

2. Instruct: *Underline the expressions that introduce the different sentence types.*

3. Elicit answers. (Answers: **reason – Firstly, In addition; evidence – According to, For example; explanation – This shows**)

Option 4

1. Follow Option 2 above.

2. Then write the following table on the board:

TS	Some retailers have greatly benefited from the rapid growth in online shopping as it has significantly increased the number of places where they can sell their goods.
1	Firstly, even retailers which cannot afford to invest in building a number of shops are able to develop their business using online shopping.
2	For instance,
3	This means that

3. Have students work in pairs or small groups to complete the type 2 and type 3 sentences.

4. Elicit answers.
   (Possible answers)
   - **2. For instance, a small retailer, which has only one actual shop, is now able to have a website that can be viewed by anyone who has internet access.**
   - **3. This means that even without having the financial resources to build shops in a number of locations, a retailer that uses the internet effectively has the potential to sell their goods to customers wherever they may be.**

Exercise 2

Option 1

1. Have students complete the exercise individually.

2. Then have students discuss their answers with a partner.

3. Elicit answers.

Option 2

1. Divide the class into pairs.

2. Have students work collaboratively to complete the exercise.

3. Elicit answers.

4. Emphasize:
   - *Any part of the "waltz" ("reason," "evidence." and "explanation") can be more than one sentence.*

3. Writing a concluding sentence

Option 1

1. Have students read the explanation.

2. Elicit:
   - *When is a concluding sentence needed?* (Answer: **When a paragraph has multiple reasons**)

- *What should the concluding sentence do?*
  (Answer: **Summarize the reasons and show how they support the writer's position**)

3. Emphasize:
   - *In most body paragraphs, there will be multiple reasons; therefore, a concluding sentence is needed to explain to readers how all of these reasons help support the thesis.*
   - *If the writer does not explain how the reasons support the position in the thesis, the reader may not be persuaded by the essay.*

Option 2

1. Follow Option 1 above.
2. Have students underline the topic and position in the thesis (page 16).
3. Elicit answer. (Answer: **"Solar power [topic] is improving people's lives in developing countries" [position]**)
4. Have students underline the words in the concluding sentence that relate to the position in the thesis.
5. Elicit answer. (Answer: **"made their lives safer"**)
6. Explain:
   - *Although the word "improve" is not used in the concluding sentence, clearly the idea of becoming "safer" is an improvement. Therefore, the concluding sentence links back to the position in the thesis, without being repetitive.*

Exercise 3

Option 1

1. Have students complete the exercise individually.
2. Then have students compare answers with a partner.
3. Elicit answers.

Option 2

1. Divide the class into pairs.
2. Have students work collaboratively to complete the exercise.
3. Elicit answers.

Option 3

1. Have students complete paragraph 1 in pairs.
2. Elicit answers.
3. Have students complete paragraph 2 individually.
4. Have students compare answers with their partner.
5. Elicit answers.
6. Emphasize:
   - *Each body paragraph must follow the "reason – evidence – explanation" pattern.*
   - *However, it does not mean that the writer only has to use one sentence for each function. For example, the evidence could be two or three sentences. The explanation could also take two or three sentences.*

- *Essentially, the writer should include enough sentences to ensure that the message is clear and convincing.*

Section 2　The concluding paragraph

Option 1

1. Have students read the explanation.
2. With books closed, elicit:
   - *What is the function of a concluding paragraph?* (Answer: **To reinforce the ideas in the essay**)
   - *Why is it so important?* (Answer: **It is the writer's last chance to make an impact on the reader.**)
   - *What should it include?* (Answer: **Restated thesis, summary of main ideas, final thought**)
   - *Should it include new ideas?* (Answer: **No**)

Option 2

1. Have students read the explanation.
2. As students are reading, draw the following table on the board:

Concluding paragraph

3. With books closed, elicit:
   - *What three types of information need to be included in the concluding paragraph?*
   (Answer)

Concluding paragraph
Restated thesis
Summary of main ideas
Final thought

4. Elicit:
   - *What is the function of a concluding paragraph?* (Answer: **To reinforce the ideas in the essay**)
   - *Why is it so important?* (Answer: **It is the writer's last chance to make an impact on the reader.**)

1. Restating the thesis

Option 1

1. Have students read the explanation.
2. With books closed, elicit:
   - *What is the purpose of a restated thesis?* (Answer: **To remind the reader of the writer's position as expressed in the thesis**)
3. Have students look at the thesis and restated thesis.

4. Elicit:
   - *What are the topic and the writer's position on this topic?*
     (Answer)
       - **The topic: "solar power"**
       - **Position: "is improving people's lives in developing countries"**
   - *Are the same words used to restate the topic and position?* (Answer: **Topic – yes; Position – no ["improving lives" "a significant difference to people's lives"; "in developing countries" "in the developing world"]**)

5. Explain:
   - *The restated thesis should not look identical to the original thesis. The writer should therefore look for ways to change:*
       - *words*
       - *sentence structure*
   - *However, the writer should be careful to not change the meaning of the restated thesis from the original thesis.*
   - *Not all of the words need to be changed. Some words are so unique and important that changing them might change the meaning or make the writing sound strange.*
   - *For example, the words "solar" and "developing" are key words, and they are not changed because there is no other simple way to write these words.*

6. Elicit:
   - *Why are the main ideas not repeated in the restated thesis?* (Answer: **Because they will be included in the "summary of main ideas"**)

Exercise 4

Option 1

1. Have students look at item 1.
2. Elicit:
   - *What is the topic and position in item 1?*
     (Answer)
       - **Topic: "Youth culture around the world"**
       - **Position: "has been significantly influenced by American youth culture"**
3. Write them on the board.
4. Elicit alternative ways to write the topic and position.
   (Possible answers)
       - **"Youth culture around the world" → young people's behavior throughout the world**
       - **"influenced by American youth culture" → affected by youth culture in the U.S.**
5. Use the new wording and write a restated thesis on the board. (Possible answer: **Youth culture in the U.S. has affected young people's behavior throughout the world.**)
6. Re-emphasize:
   - *The structure of the sentence, as well as the vocabulary, could also be changed.*
7. Have students complete item 2 in pairs.
8. Then have pairs swap their answer with another pair.

9. Elicit answers and comment on how well the vocabulary and structure have been changed.
10. Have students do item 3 individually.
11. Have students swap item 3 with a partner for feedback.
12. Elicit answers. Again, comment on how well the vocabulary and structure have been changed.

Option 2

1. Divide the class into pairs.
2. For each thesis statement, have pairs identify the topic and position.
3. Have pairs brainstorm ways to restate these.
4. Then have pairs swap their restated theses with another pair to compare.
5. Elicit answers. Comment on how well the vocabulary and structure have been changed.

2. Summarizing the main points

Option 1

1. Have students read the explanation.
2. With books closed, elicit:
   - *Why is it necessary to summarize each body paragraph's main idea?* (Answer: **To remind the reader of how the position has been supported**)
3. Emphasize:
   - *As with the restated thesis, the wording of the summary of the main ideas should not be identical to the wording in the body paragraphs.*
   - *The writer should therefore look for ways to change:*
       - *words*
       - *sentence structure*
   - *However, the writer should be careful to not change the meaning expressed in the body paragraphs.*
   - *Not all of the words need to be changed. Some words are so unique and important that changing them might change the meaning or make the writing sound strange.*

Option 2

1. Have students look at the concluding paragraph at the bottom of page 6.
2. In pairs, have students discuss:
   - *How is the wording in the summarized main points different from the wording in the body paragraphs?*
   - *How is the wording in the summarized main points the same as the wording in the body paragraphs?*
3. Elicit answers.
   (Possible answers)
   - **Some words changed (e.g., "dependable," "stable" → "efficient"; "communicate with the world" → "global communication"; "independence" → "take control")**
   - **Some sentence structures changed**

3. Writing a final thought

Option 1

1. Have students read the explanation.
2. With books closed, elicit:
   - *What are the different types of final thoughts?* (Answer: **Opinion or judgment, solution or recommendation, prediction or speculation**)
   - *What must a final thought not do?* (Answer: **It must not introduce new information.**)

Option 2

1. Follow Option 1 above.
2. Divide the class into pairs.
3. Have each pair write a "prediction" type of final thought for the example paragraph.
4. Have pairs swap their final thought with another pair and compare.
5. Elicit a few answers. Comment on:
   - language use
   - how closely it relates to the essay's topic and main ideas.

> **Exercise 5**

1. Have students complete the exercise individually.
2. Then have students compare answers with a partner.
3. Elicit answers.

> **Exercise 6**

Option 1

1. Have students complete the exercise individually.
2. Then have students compare answers with a partner.
3. Elicit answers.
4. For each question, after getting the right answer, elicit:
   - *Why are the other answers incorrect?* (See answer key.)

Option 2

1. Follow Option 1 above.
2. Then, in pairs, have students write an alternative final thought for each of the paragraphs.
3. Have pairs swap their new final thoughts with another pair for feedback.
4. Elicit answers. Comment on:
   - language use
   - how closely it relates to the essay's topic and main ideas.

> **Section 3** Outlining an essay

Option 1

1. Have students read the explanation.
2. With books closed, elicit:
   - *Why is writing an essay outline important?* (Answer: **An outline helps the writer to stay focused and write a logical, well-organized essay.**)
   - *What should be included in an essay outline?* (Answer: **Thesis statement, topic sentences, supporting points**)

Option 2

1. Divide the class into small groups.
2. Have students discuss the following questions:
   - *Why is writing an essay outline important?* (Answer: **An outline helps the writer to stay focused and write a logical, well-organized essay.**)
   - *What information should be included in an essay outline?* (Answer: **Thesis statement, topic sentences, supporting points – the more details the better**)
3. Elicit answers.
4. Have students read the explanation for a fuller understanding.
5. Confirm if the previous answers are correct.
6. Emphasize:
   - *The more information that is included in an outline, the easier it will be to write a well-organized and logical essay.*
   - *An outline should not be thought of as a final plan for the essay. It can be changed.*

> **Exercise 7**

Option 1

1. Divide the class into pairs.
2. Have students work collaboratively to complete the exercise.
3. Elicit answers.

Option 2

1. Have students complete the exercise individually.
2. Then have students compare answers with a partner.
3. Elicit answers.

UNIT 1

Part 3
Improving your work

Section 1   Revising and editing

Option 1

1. Have students read the explanation.
2. Elicit:
   - *What is the difference between revising and editing?* (Answer: **Revising is changing the content and organization; editing is changing vocabulary, grammar, and form of sentences,**)
   - *Why are revising and editing important?* (Answer: **They make the writer look at the essay in a critical way; this should improve the quality of the essay and develop the writer's ability to evaluate writing.**)
   - *What is peer editing?* (Answer: **Editing and revising the essays of classmates**)
   - *How many drafts of an essay should you write?* (Answer: **At least 3**)

Option 2

1. Divide the class into pairs or small groups.
2. Have students discuss the following questions:
   - *Why is it important to spend time revising and editing your essay after you have written it?* (Possible answer: **Initial drafts almost always have mistakes or could be written better; therefore, writers should take time to revise and edit to improve their writing.**)
   - *When making changes, should you mainly focus on problems with grammar and vocabulary?* (Possible answer: **No. The content and organization should also be changed.**)
   - *Why is it useful to get feedback on your essay from other students?* (Possible answer: **They are more likely to read it objectively; they may find problems that you have missed.**)
   - *Why is it useful to give feedback on other students' essays?* (Possible answer: **It will encourage you to think objectively about what makes good writing.**)
   - *How many times should you rewrite an essay?* (Possible answer: **At least 3**)
3. Elicit answers.
4. Then have students read the explanation for a fuller understanding.
5. Emphasize:
   - *Revising and editing is not done only by students. Any published piece of writing (articles, books, etc.) will have been through this process several times before being published.*

1. Writing for a reader
Option 1

1. Divide the class into small groups.
2. Have students brainstorm:
   - *What will make a good impression on a person who reads your essay?*
3. Elicit answers and write them on the board.
4. Have students look at the list at the top of page 24 in the textbook and compare it with the list on the board.

Option 2

1. Have students read the explanation on page 24 of the textbook.
2. In pairs and with books closed, have students recall:
   - *What will readers expect of your essay?*
3. Elicit answers.

2. Academic tone
Option 1

1. Have students read the explanation.
2. Write the following sentences on the board:
   I think that we need to protect the environment.
   You can purchase products made with animal fur in many large department stores.
   Learning a foreign language can be a great way to improve your employment prospects.
3. In pairs, have students rewrite the sentences with a more academic tone.
4. Elicit answers.
   (Possible answers)
   - **The environment needs to be protected.**
   - **Products made with animal fur can be purchased in many large department stores.**
   - **Employment prospects can be significantly improved by learning a foreign language.**
5. Emphasize:
   - *Students should pay close attention to the information presented in this section. Making these mistakes is extremely common in student writing.*
   - *Making these mistakes creates a negative impression on the reader and means your essay will be less effective.*

Option 2

1. Follow Option 1 above.
2. Have students write five sentences that use first- or second-person pronouns (e.g., *I, we, you*), or emotional words (e.g., *the best, great, terrific, worst, stupid*).

3. Have students swap their five sentences with a partner.

4. Then have students rewrite their partner's sentences with a more academic tone.

Note: Further explanations and exercises to improve academic tone can be found in Appendix A in the textbook.

Section 2 — Revising the content and organization

1. Have students read the explanation and editing checklist.

2. Then have students, in pairs or small groups and with books closed, recall what they read.

3. Elicit answers to the following:
   - *What are questions you can ask about the whole essay?*
   - *What are questions you can ask about the introductory paragraph?*
   - *What are questions you can ask about the body paragraphs?*
   - *What are questions you can ask about the concluding paragraph?*
   (Answers: See textbook page 25, checklist)

Exercise 1

Option 1

1. Have students read the draft.

2. Then have students individually revise the draft using the checklist.

3. Divide the class into pairs or small groups.

4. Have students compare the revisions that they have made. Remind students to comment on what is successful in the draft and why, as well as what needs to be improved.

5. Elicit answers.

Option 2

1. Have students read the draft.

2. Divide the class into pairs or small groups.

3. Have the pairs/groups work collaboratively to revise the draft using the checklist.

4. Have each pair/group swap their revised draft with another pair/group to compare the revisions they have made.

5. Elicit answers.

Section 3 — Editing grammatical errors

Option 1

1. Have students read the explanations (pages 27–29).

2. Have students, in pairs or small groups and with books closed, recall what they read.

3. Elicit:
   - *When should you use a comma?* (Answer: See points on pages 27–28.)
   - *What is a relative clause?* (Answer: **Clause that modifies the noun before or after it**)
   - *What is the difference between a restrictive and a non-restrictive relative clause?* (Answer)
     - **Restrictive: information is essential; no commas necessary**
     - **Non-restrictive: information is not essential; commas necessary**
   - *What is an appositive?* (Answer: **A shortened form of a non-restrictive relative clause**)

4. Write the following sentences on the board:
   Many people practice yoga to relax.
   Facebook has become extremely popular among young people.

5. Elicit:
   - *How can these sentences be modified to include more information?* (Answer: See the example sentences in the middle of page 28.)
   - *When should you use a colon?* (Answer: See the points on page 28.)
   - *When should you use a semicolon?* (Answer: See the points on page 28.)

Option 2

1. Have students read the explanations (pages 27–29).

2. Write the following on the board:
   The Effects Of Global Warming On The Polar Ice Caps.
   Protecting the environment is crucial to maintaining living standards yet many people do not recognize this.
   Firstly the increase in the popularity of football has led to professional players receiving higher salaries.
   The New Deal which was implemented between 1933 and 1936 had a huge impact on American society.

3. In pairs, have students correct the sentences. Make sure students understand that the first sentence is an essay title.

4. Elicit answers.
   (Possible answers)
   - **The Effects of Global Warming on the Polar Ice Caps**
   - **Protecting the environment is crucial to maintaining living standards, yet many people do not recognize this.**
   - **Firstly, the increase in the popularity of football has led to professional players receiving higher salaries.**
   - **The New Deal, which was implemented between 1933 and 1936, had a huge impact on American society.**

Option 3

1. Write the following sentences from the textbook on the board.

   The Relationship Between The Ancient And Modern Olympics

   Many high school students spend their time after school at shopping malls, fast food restaurants and cafes.

   First poverty is not a problem only in poor countries.

   Facebook a social networking service on the internet has become extremely popular among young people.

   When a person's family member passes away, it is said that they go through the stages of grief. Denial, anger, bargaining, depression, and acceptance.

2. In pairs, have students correct the sentences. Make sure students understand that the first sentence is an essay title.

3. Then have students check their answers against the examples in the textbook.

Exercise 2

Option 1

1. Have students complete the exercise individually.

2. Then have students compare answers with a partner.

3. Elicit answers.

Option 2

1. Divide the class into pairs.

2. Have students work collaboratively to complete the exercise.

3. Elicit answers.

Note: Further explanations and exercises on punctuation can be found in Appendix F in the textbook.

3. Sentences and words

Option 1

1. Have students read the explanations and examples (pages 29–30).

2. Have students, in pairs or small groups and with books closed, recall what they read.

3. Elicit:
   - *What are some common problems with sentences and words in an essay?* (Answer: See the points on pages 29–30.)

Option 2

1. Write the following sentences from the textbook on the board:

   People are attracted to new things, cell phones companies often upgrade existing models.

   Some people like to shop at Gucci, and they like to shop at Saks, and shop at Tiffany.

   Once a month, he go to the museum to see new exhibitions.

   The first Europeans who come to New York buy Manhattan Island from the Native Americans for only $24.

   In this global world, people can enjoy diversity cultures.

2. Have students work with a partner to correct them.

3. Then have students check their answers against the examples in the textbook.

Exercise 3

Option 1

1. Have students complete the exercise individually.

2. Then have students compare answers with a partner.

3. Elicit answers.

Option 2

1. Divide the class into pairs.

2. Have students work collaboratively to complete the exercise.

3. Elicit answers.

UNIT 2

Part 1
Introduction to research and citation

Finding sources for academic essays

Option 1

1. In pairs or groups, have students discuss:
   - *Why is research an important part of academic writing?*
   - *What are some good sources when conducting research?*
   - *How can you tell if source material is reliable?*

2. Elicit answers.
   (Possible answers)
   - **It increases the writer's knowledge of a topic, and provides specific evidence that can be used in the essay.**
   - **Books, magazines, newspapers, journals**
   - **Check authority, purpose, relevance**

3. Have students read the explanation in the textbook.

Option 2

1. Have students read the explanation.

2. Have students, in pairs or small groups and with books closed, recall what they read.

3. Elicit:
   - *Why is research an important part of academic writing?* (Answer: **It increases the writer's knowledge of a topic, and provides specific evidence that can be used in the essay.**)
   - *What are some good sources when conducting research?* (Answer: **Books, periodicals, indexes, databases, reports**)
   - *What are the four criteria that should be used to check the suitability of source material?* (Answer: **Authority, purpose, intended audience, relevance**)
   - *Why is it important to keep a record of the sources that you may wish to use in your essay?* (Answer: **It will be needed when writing a Works Cited list.**)

Exercise 1

Option 1

1. Have students work in pairs to complete the exercise.

2. Elicit answers.

Option 2

1. Follow Option 1 above.

2. Then write the following sources on the board:
   A blog written by Bill Gates.
   An academic article titled "The Importance of Business Ethics in Building a Company" which was written in 1946.

3. In pairs or small groups, have students discuss:
   - *How suitable are these sources for an academic essay on starting an IT company?*

4. Elicit answers.
   (Answers)
   - **Although a blog, this would appear to be a suitable source because it was written by someone with great authority in the field.**
   - **Although an academic article, this would appear to be unsuitable due to its having been written long before the birth of the IT industry.**

5. Emphasize:
   - *The suitability of source material will depend on the essay topic.*

Plagiarism

Option 1

1. Have students read the explanation.

2. Elicit:
   - *What is plagiarism?* (Answer: **When other people's work is falsely presented as the essay writer's own**)
   - *What is necessary to avoid plagiarism?* (Answer: **Using a quotation, paraphrase, or summary AND citation**)

Option 2

1. In pairs or small groups, have students discuss:
   - *What is plagiarism?*
   - *What is the penalty for plagiarism at many universities?*

2. Elicit answers.
   (Answers)
   - **When other people's work is falsely presented as the essay writer's own**
   - **Many universities have zero tolerance for plagiarism and will expel students caught doing it.**

3. Have students read the explanation in the textbook.

4. Elicit:
   - *What is necessary to avoid plagiarism?* (Answer: **Use a quotation, paraphrase, or summary AND citation**)

5. Emphasize:
    *   *Plagiarism is a serious offense in the academic world.*
    *   *The following sections in the textbook will cover what is needed in order to use outside sources without committing plagiarism.*

Section 3 — Using outside sources in academic essays

Option 1

1. Have students read the explanations (pages 33–35).
2. As students are reading, draw the following table on the board:

	Definition	When to use
Quotation		
Paraphrasing		
Summarizing		

3. Have students, in pairs or small groups and with books closed, recall what they read.
4. Elicit answers to complete the table.

	Definition	When to use
Quotation	Use of the exact words from another text.	The author of the quote is an authority on the essay topic. The words make a strong impression on the reader.
Paraphrasing	Putting information from another text into your own words.	The writer wants to use all the information from a passage. Only suitable for short pieces of information.
Summarizing	Making a summary of information from another text.	The writer only wants to use the main ideas from a source. Suitable when including information from longer sources.

Option 2

1. Divide the class into groups of three.

2. Have students draw the table as in Option 1 above.
3. Then in each group:
    *   Have one student read the section on quotations (page 34).
    *   Have one student read the section on paraphrasing (page 34).
    *   Have one student read the section on summarizing (page 35).
4. When done, have students close their textbooks and work collaboratively to complete the table.
5. Elicit answers.
6. Emphasize:
    *   *The following sections of the textbook will cover how to use each of these skills.*

Section 4 — Shared language

Option 1

1. Explain:
    *   *When paraphrasing or summarizing, it is necessary to change some of the vocabulary, but not all of it. Therefore, it is necessary to identify which words/phrases cannot be changed.*
    *   *Vocabulary that should not be changed is called "shared language."*
2. To demonstrate the idea of shared language, elicit from students:
    *   *What is another way to write "octopus"?* (Possible answer: **An eight-legged creature that lives in the sea**)
3. Emphasize:
    *   *This is clearly not an appropriate way to change the word. It is inefficient and unnecessarily long. There is no simple way to change the word because it is a common noun.*
4. Have students read the explanation.
5. Elicit from students:
    *   *What types of words or phrases are usually considered shared language?* (Answer: **Proper nouns, common nouns, dates and figures, specialized language**)

Option 2

1. Have students read the explanation.
2. With books closed, elicit:
    *   *What is shared language?* (Answer: **Words from the original source that should remain the same**)
    *   *What types of words or phrases are usually considered shared language?* (Answer: **Proper nouns, common nouns, dates and figures, specialized language**)
    *   *How can you determine what is shared language?* (Answer: **If the word or phrase doesn't belong to one writer, is used with the same meaning by everyone, and changing the word may make the wording strange.**)

3. Emphasize:
   - When paraphrasing or summarizing, it is necessary to change some of the vocabulary, but not all of it. Therefore, it is necessary to identify which words/phrases cannot be changed.

Exercise 2

1. Have students complete the exercise individually.
2. Then have students compare answers with a partner.
3. Elicit answers.

Section 5 Writing a paraphrase

Option 1

1. Elicit from students:
   - *What is paraphrasing?* (Answer: **Putting information from another text into your own words**)
2. Divide the class into pairs (Student A and Student B).
3. In each pair, have Student A read the six steps; have Student B keep their textbook closed.
4. While Student A is reading, have Student B draw the following table:

Step 1	
Step 2	
Step 3	
Step 4	
Step 5	
Step 6	

5. With books closed, have Student A explain the paraphrasing steps to Student B. Student B should complete the table.
6. Have pairs compare the information in Student B's table with the information in the textbook.

Option 2

1. Have students read the explanation.
2. As students are reading, draw the following table on the board:

How to Paraphrase	
Step 1	
Step 2	
Step 3	
Step 4	
Step 5	
Step 6	

3. Have students, in pairs or small groups and with books closed, recall what they read.
4. Elicit answers to complete the table.
5. Emphasize:
   When paraphrasing:
   - *Change the vocabulary and structure of the original source, but do not change the meaning.*
   - *Do not use more than three words in a row from the original.*
   - *Make the paraphrase approximately the same length as the original.*

Exercise 3

1. Have students complete the exercise individually.
2. Then have students discuss their answers in small groups. Make sure students discuss why the other options are unsuitable. (See Answer Key.)
3. Elicit answers.

Exercise 4

Option 1

1. Have students read item 1.
2. Elicit:
   - *What is the shared language?*
3. Write the answers on the board. (Possible answers: **Caribbean, the United Kingdom, racism, British society**)
4. Elicit the main points. Write these on the board in point form.
   (Possible answers)
   - **Immigrants from Caribbean started to arrive in UK post-WW2.**
   - **Reasons: better life and fill job vacancies**
   - **Problems: racism, finding employment, finding place to live**
   - **Present situation: part of British society**
5. Use these notes to write the paraphrase on the board. (See Answer Key.)
6. Have students work in pairs or small groups to paraphrase item 2.
7. Instruct:
   - *Only one student has to write.*
   - *The others should help with organization, spelling, and grammar.*
8. Have groups swap their paraphrase with another pair/group to compare.
9. Have students give feedback to each other on these questions:
   - *Is plagiarism avoided?*
   - *Is the meaning the same as the original?*
10. Elicit answers.
11. Have students complete item 3 individually.
12. Have students swap their paraphrase with a partner to compare.

13. Have students give feedback to each other on these questions:
    - *Is plagiarism avoided?*
    - *Is the meaning the same as the original?*
14. Elicit answers.

Option 2

1. Follow Option 1 steps 1–4 above.
2. Have students complete items 2 and 3 individually.
3. Have students swap their paraphrases with a partner to compare.
4. Have students give feedback to each other on these questions:
    - *Is plagiarism avoided?*
    - *Is the meaning the same as the original?*
5. Elicit answers.

Note: This is a difficult skill for students. Perfect paraphrases should not be expected. The goal is for students to become aware of the types of changes that need to be carried out when paraphrasing.

Option 3

1. Have students complete items 1, 2, and 3 individually.
2. Then have students compare answers in pairs or groups.

Section 6   Writing a summary

Option 1

1. Elicit from students:
    - *What is summarizing?* (Answer: **Making a summary of information from another text**)
2. Divide the class into pairs (Student A and Student B).
3. Have Student A in each pair read the five steps; have Student B keep their textbook closed.
4. While Student A is reading, have Student B draw the following table:

Step 1	
Step 2	
Step 3	
Step 4	
Step 5	

5. With textbooks closed, have Student A explain the summarizing steps to Student B. Student B should complete the table.
6. Have pairs compare the information in Student B's table with the information in the textbook.

Option 2

1. Have students read the explanation.
2. As students are reading, draw the following table on the board:

How to Summarize	
Step 1	
Step 2	
Step 3	
Step 4	
Step 5	

3. Have students, in pairs or small groups and with books closed, recall what they read.
4. Elicit answers to complete the table.
5. Emphasize:
    - *When summarizing, change the vocabulary and sentence structure, but do not change the meaning from the original.*
    - *A summary should only be one or two sentences. Usually, one long sentence is enough.*

Exercise 5

1. Have students complete the exercise individually.
2. Then have students discuss their answers in small groups.
3. Elicit answers.

Exercise 6

Option 1

1. Have students read item 1.
2. Elicit the shared language from the class. Write it on the board. (Possible answers: **Indigenous people, defined, group, language**)
3. Elicit the main points from the class. Write these on the board in point form. (Possible answer: **Indigenous people = group from a colonized place, have a different way of life and language from colonizers**)
4. Use these notes to write the summary on the board. (See Answer Key.)
5. Have students work in pairs or small groups to summarize item 2.
6. Instruct:
    - *Only one student has to write.*
    - *The others should help with organization, spelling, and grammar.*
7. Have pairs/groups swap their summary with another pair/group to compare.
8. Have students give feedback to each other on these questions:
    - *Is plagiarism avoided?*
    - *Are only the main ideas included?*
    - *Is the meaning the same as the original?*
9. Elicit answers.
10. Have students complete item 3 individually.
11. Have students swap their summary with a partner to compare.

12. Have students give feedback to each other on these questions:
    - Is plagiarism avoided?
    - Are only the main ideas included?
    - Is the meaning the same as the original?

13. Elicit answers.

Note: This is a difficult skill for students. Perfect summaries should not be expected. The goal is for students to become aware of the types of changes that need to be carried out when summarizing.

Option 2

1. Follow Option 1 steps 1–4.

2. Have students complete items 2 and 3 individually.

3. Have students swap their summary with a partner to compare.

4. Have students give feedback to each other on these questions:
    - *Is plagiarism avoided?*
    - *Are only the main ideas included?*
    - *Is the meaning the same as the original?*

5. Elicit answers.

Option 3

1. Have students complete the questions individually.

2. Then have students compare answers in pairs or groups.

UNIT 2

Part 2
In-text citation and the Works Cited list

Introduction

1. Have students read the explanation.

2. Have students, in pairs or small groups and with books closed, recall what they read.

3. Elicit:
   - *What are the two parts of citation?* (Answer: **In-text citation and a Works Cited list**)
   - *Why is citation necessary?* (Answer: **So that if readers want to, they can find the information in the original source, and in order to avoid plagiarism**)
   - *What information about the source of the information is usually included in an in-text citation?* (Answer: **Author's last name and page number**)
   - *How is the Works Cited list organized?* (Answer: **Alphabetically**)
   - *Where is the Works Cited list located?* (Answer: **On a separate page at the end of an essay**)
   - *What information is in a Works Cited list?* (Answer: **Complete information on where each source can be found**)

4. Emphasize:
   - *There are a number of different citation styles. This textbook uses Modern Language Association (MLA).*

Section 2 Citing sources in the essay text

1. Common knowledge

Option 1

1. Have students read the explanation.

2. Test students' understanding of the idea of "common knowledge" by asking:
   - *Do the following sentences require citation?*
     - *The only time that England has won the FIFA World Cup was in 1966.*
     - *The capital of Zimbabwe is Harare.*

3. Explain:
   - *These sentences are considered common knowledge because they are established facts. Their accuracy is accepted by the majority of people. Therefore, they would not need citation.*

Option 2

1. Have students read the explanation.

2. With books closed, elicit:
   - *When is citation required?* (Answer: **When using a quotation, paraphrase, summary, or information that is not widely known**)

   - *When is citation not required?* (Answer: **If the ideas and opinions are the essay writer's own, or if they are considered common knowledge**)
   - *What is common knowledge?* (Students are likely to *incorrectly* answer: "Something that most people know.")

3. Test the validity of this last answer by asking:
   - *How many times has England won the FIFA World Cup?* (Answer: **Once, in 1966**)
   - *What is the capital of Zimbabwe?* (Answer: **Harare**)
   - *Are these pieces of information considered common knowledge?* (The students are likely to *incorrectly* answer: "No, because many people in the class did not know them.")

4. Explain:
   - *They are considered common knowledge because they are established facts. Their accuracy is accepted by the majority of people. Therefore, they would not need citation.*

5. Have students read the examples in the textbook (page 42) for further clarification.

6. Emphasize:
   - *If the writer is not sure whether or not the information is considered common knowledge, it is better to include citation.*

Exercise 1

Option 1

1. Have students complete the exercise individually.

2. Then have students discuss their answers in pairs.

3. Elicit answers.

Option 2

1. Divide the class into pairs.

2. Have students work collaboratively to complete the exercise.

3. Elicit answers.

2. Using in-text citation

As there is a lot of information on "Using in-text citation," the following procedure has been divided into two parts.

Part 1

1. Have students read the explanation from pages 43 to the end of the section on "Pattern 2" (middle of page 45).

2. Have students, in pairs or small groups and with books closed, recall what they read.

3. Elicit:
   - *What are the two key elements of in-text citation?* (Answer: **Author and page number**)

- *What are two in-text citation patterns that can be used?*
  (Answer)
  - **Pattern 1: author + quote/paraphrase/ summary + (page number)**
  - **Pattern 2: quote/paraphrase/summary + (author's last name/organization name + page number)**
- *What are five common reporting verbs?*
  (Possible answer: See list, top of page 44)
- *Why is the choice of reporting verb important?*
  (Possible answer: **It expresses the author's position on the information.**)
- Why might it be necessary to add authority to a source? (Answer: **The source may be unknown to the reader.**)
- How can the writer add authority to a source? (Answer: **By describing the source's position or background**)

Part 2

4. Have students read the explanation on "Sources with no author" (middle of page 45) to the end of the section on "Secondhand information" (middle of page 46).

5. Have students, in pairs or small groups and with books closed, recall what they read.

6. Elicit:
   - *What information should be included in-text if the source has no named author?*
     (Answer)
     - **Pattern 1: The entire title of the source in quotation marks**
     - **Pattern 2: The first, or first few, content words of the title in quotation marks**
   - *What information should be included in-text if the source has no page numbers?* (Answer: **Only the first piece of information from the Works Cited list, usually the author's last name**)
   - *What is "secondhand information"?* (Answer: **Information from a source that is taken from another source**)
   - *If "secondhand information" is used, how should it be cited?*
     (Answers)
     - **Cite both the secondhand source and the original source; often the original source is mentioned in the sentence; e.g., from the textbook:**
       "James Stuart, Assistant Bureau Manager at the Ministry of Energy, said . . ."
     - **At the end of the quote in parentheses: qtd. in + author's last name + page number; e.g., from the textbook:**
       (qtd. in Moore 76)

Exercise 2

Option 1

1. Have students complete the exercise individually.
2. Have students discuss their answers in pairs.
3. Elicit answers.

Option 2

1. Divide the class into pairs.
2. Have students work collaboratively to complete the exercise.
3. Elicit answers.

Exercise 3

Option 1

1. Elicit from students:
   - *What are the three different types of supporting sentences?* (Answer: **1 – state a reason; 2 – provide evidence; 3 – provide an explanation**)
     Note: This is a review of "the waltz" on page 14.

2. Explain that the paragraph in Exercise 3 is missing its Type 2 sentences (the evidence).

3. Divide the class into pairs or groups.

4. Have students read the thesis statement, body paragraph, and evidence.

5. Have the pairs/groups discuss:
   - *What is the logical place for each piece of evidence?*
   - *How should the evidence be cited appropriately?*

6. When done, have a student from one pair/group swap books with a student from another pair/ group and compare.

7. Elicit answers.

Option 2

1. Follow steps 1 and 2 from Option 1 above.
2. Have students complete the exercise individually.
3. Have students swap with a partner to compare.
4. Have students give feedback by asking:
   - *Is each piece of evidence in a logical place?*
   - *Is the evidence cited appropriately?*
5. Elicit answers.
6. Emphasize:
   - *Accurately integrating outside evidence is a key part of academic writing.*
   - *How the evidence helps support the controlling idea must be explained, which is the Type 3 sentence.*

Section 3 Creating a Works Cited list

Option 1

1. Have students read the explanation on pages 51–52.

2. Have students, in pairs or small groups and with books closed, recall what they read.

3. Elicit:
   - *In a Works Cited list:*
     - *What information do you need from a book?*
       (Answer: **Author, title, city published, publisher, year of publication**)

- *What information do you need from a publication?* (Answer: **Author, article title, journal name, date of publication, pages**)
- *What dates do you need if the source is from an electronic newspaper or a website?* (Answer: **date of publication and date of access**)
- *For a government website, what information should come first in the entry?* (Answer: **The country's name**)
- *If there is information missing, such as the author's name, what should you do?* (Answer: **Cite the information which is available**)
- *What are some further rules regarding a Works Cited page?* (Answer: See list, bottom of page 52)

4. Have students look at the Works Cited list on page 53.

5. Elicit:
   - *How is this Works Cited list ordered?* (Answer: **Alphabetically**)

6. Emphasize:
   - *All Works Cited lists should be ordered alphabetically.*

Option 2

1. There are a lot of complicated rules in this section. Have students read the rules at their own pace, then go on to do Exercise 4 to test their understanding of the rules.

2. Explain that students do not need to memorize these rules – the important thing is that they refer to them when creating a Works Cited list.

Exercise 4

Option 1

1. Have students complete the exercise individually.

2. Have students compare their Works Cited list in pairs or groups.

3. Have students compare their Works Cited list with the model. (See Answer Key.)

Option 2

1. Divide the class into pairs or small groups.

2. Assign each pair/group one of the sources (as much as possible, assign a different source for each pair/group).

3. Have students work collaboratively to complete the Works Cited entry for their assigned source.

4. When done, have individual students from each pair/group come to the board to write their Works Cited entry so that eventually the entries for all of the sources are on the board.

5. Go to each entry on the board and elicit:
   - *Is this entry OK?*
   If not, elicit corrections.

6. When done with all of the entries, elicit:
   - *In a Works Cited list, what should the first entry be?*

   When the correct answer is given, write *1* next to that entry. (See Answer Key.)

7. Then elicit:
   - *What should the next entry be?*

   When the correct answer is given, write *2* next to that entry.

8. Repeat step 7 for the rest of the entries, numbering *3* and *4*.

9. Emphasize:
   - *Many software applications and online services will automatically create Works Cited lists.*
   - *The MLA rules are updated periodically; therefore, it is important to refer to official MLA resources for the most up-to-date versions.*

UNIT 3

Part 1
Developing arguments

Section 1 — An argumentative essay

Option 1

1. In pairs or small groups, have students discuss:
   - *What is an argumentative essay?*
   - *What topics have you written argumentative essays about?*

2. Elicit answers.
   (Possible answers)
   - **Presents and supports a position on a topic**
   - **Answers will vary.**

3. Then have students discuss:
   - *What should you do in your writing to convince a reader to accept your argument?*

4. Elicit answers. (Possible answers: **Explain your argument logically, include cited evidence, include counter-arguments and rebuttals**)

5. Have students read the explanation.

6. Elicit:
   - *Does the book's information match what you discussed about argumentative essays?*

Option 2

1. Have students read the explanation.

2. With books closed, elicit:
   - *What is an argumentative essay?* (Answer: **Presents and supports a position on a topic**)
   - *What should you do in your writing to convince a reader to accept your argument?*
     (Answer: **Explain your opinion logically, include authoritative evidence, include counter-arguments and rebuttals**)
   - *What are the steps you should take before you start writing your essay?*
     (Answer)
     1. Read the question; take a position
     2. Do research
     3. Consider counter-arguments and rebuttals
     4. Write a thesis and outline

3. Emphasize:
   - *Taking a position does not always simply mean something is right or wrong, good or bad, better or worse.*
   - *Taking a position could also mean claiming something is true about a subject, and then presenting evidence to support that claim.*

Exercise 1

Option 1

1. Have students read the two questions.

2. To review thesis statements (page 7), elicit:
   - *Where can the answers be found?* (Answer: **In the thesis statement, which is the final sentence of the introductory paragraph**)

3. Have students look at the thesis, then elicit answers to the two textbook questions.

Option 2

1. Follow Option 1 above.

2. Then elicit:
   - *What other information is included in the thesis statement?* (Answer: **The main ideas that will be used to support the writer's position**)
   - *What will the first body paragraph be about?* (Answer: **"offering a comprehensive overview of complex topics"**)
   - *Based on the main ideas mentioned in the thesis, what specific information do you expect to read about in the rest of the essay?* (Answers will vary.)

3. Have students read the whole essay.

4. Then elicit:
   - *Did any of the information you read about match what you predicted would be in the essay?*

5. Emphasize:
   - *The thesis statement should always contain the essay topic and the writer's position on the topic.*
   - *Listing the main ideas in the thesis will help readers predict what information will be included in the essay.*

Option 3

1. Have students read the essay.

2. In pairs, with books closed, have students:
   - Answer the two questions.
   - Summarize what they read.

3. Elicit answers to the questions and a summary of the essay.

4. Then, in pairs or small groups, have students discuss:
   - *Do you agree with the writer's position?*

5. Elicit answers.

Section 2 — Dealing with counter-arguments

Option 1

1. Have students read the explanation.

2. With books closed, elicit:
   - *Why is it necessary to include a counter-argument in argumentative essays?* (Answer: **It shows that the writer has considered all sides of the issue. It makes the essay more objective.**)
   - *Why is it necessary to rebut them?* (Answer: **If you don't, they will weaken your position.**)
3. Have students open their books and read the capital punishment example.
4. Elicit:
   - *Why is this a good rebuttal?* (Answer: **It directly attacks the point raised in the counter-argument.**)

Option 2

1. Follow Option 1 above.
2. Have each student:
   - Write another argument against abolishing the death penalty.
   - Swap their argument with a partner.
   - Write a rebuttal to their partner's counter-argument.

Option 3

1. Follow Option 1 above.
2. Divide the class into two halves (Sides A and B).
3. In pairs, have students on Side A brainstorm reasons in favor of abolishing the death penalty.
4. In pairs, have students on Side B brainstorm reasons against abolishing the death penalty.
5. Then re-organize the class:
   - Have students form groups of four.
   - Each group should have two students from Side A and two students from Side B.
6. Have the groups debate the issue of abolishing the death penalty.

Exercise 2

Option 1

1. Have students read item 1.
2. Elicit:
   - *What is the key point in the argument?* (Answer: **"Students can learn the language and culture of a different country"**)
3. Emphasize:
   - *The counter-argument must focus on this point.*
4. Have students:
   - Write a counter-argument for item 1.
   - Swap with a partner.
   - Give feedback to their partner answering the question:
     - *Does the counter-argument focus on the point of the writer's argument?*
5. Elicit answers.
6. Repeat the process for items 2 and 3.

Option 2

1. Divide the class into pairs.
2. Have students work collaboratively to complete the exercise.
3. Then have each pair swap their answers with another pair.
4. Have the pairs give feedback to each other answering the question:
   - *Do the counter-arguments focus on the point of the writer's argument?*
5. Elicit answers.

Section 3 — Presenting a strong rebuttal

Option 1

1. Elicit:
   - *Why is it necessary to rebut a counter-argument?* (Answer: **To convince the reader that the writer's own argument is stronger**)
2. Have students:
   - Read the example of an ineffective rebuttal.
   - Underline the key words in the counter-argument and the ineffective rebuttal. (Answer: **Counter-argument – "it is filled with incorrect, biased information"; Rebuttal – "the number of entries . . . continues to increase"**)
3. Elicit:
   - *Why is this rebuttal ineffective?* (Answer: **There is no relationship between "incorrect, biased" and the number of entries increasing; the entries could still be incorrect.**)
4. Then have students:
   - Read the example of an effective rebuttal.
   - Underline the key words in the counter-argument and the effective rebuttal. (Answer: **Counter-argument – "it is filled with incorrect, biased information"; Rebuttal – "quickly remedy inaccurate information; controversial entries can be tagged . . ."**)
5. Elicit:
   - *Why is this rebuttal effective?* (Answer: **The two aspects of the counter-argument are shown to be insignificant to the writer's position, as Wikipedia has taken effective action to deal with the problems raised in the counter-argument.**)

Option 2

1. Have students read the explanation and examples.
2. Have students, in pairs or small groups and with books closed, recall what they read.
3. Elicit:
   - *Why is it necessary to rebut a counter-argument?* (Answer: **To convince the reader that the writer's own argument is stronger.**)
   - *Why is the first rebuttal ineffective?* (Answer: **There is no relationship between "incorrect, biased" and the number of entries increasing; the entries could still be incorrect.**)

- *Why is the second rebuttal effective?* (Answer: **The two aspects of the counter-argument are shown to be insignificant to the writer's position, as Wikipedia has taken effective action to deal with the problems raised in the counter-argument.**)

4. Emphasize:
   - *In order or effectively rebut a counter-argument, the writer must focus on the specific point raised in the counter-argument. The writer must show why the counter-argument is incorrect or weaker than the writer's own position.*

Exercise 3

Option 1

1. Divide the class into pairs.
2. Have pairs work collaboratively to complete the two questions.
3. Elicit answers.

Option 2

1. Have students complete the exercise individually.
2. Then have students compare answers with a partner.
3. Elicit answers.

Option 3

1. Follow Option 1 or 2 above.
2. Also instruct students:
   - *Underline the key words in the counter-arguments and the effective rebuttals.* (Answers)
     - 1. Counter-argument – "<u>freedom to talk about personal interests</u>"; rebuttal – "<u>nothing more than casual conversations about familiar topics</u>"
     - 2. Counter-argument – "<u>better understanding of their strengths and weaknesses</u>"; rebuttal – "<u>same level,</u>" "<u>share the same problems,</u>" "<u>guided by the teacher, can help each other improve</u>"

Exercise 4

Option 1

1. Have students:
   - Write rebuttals to the counter-arguments they wrote in Exercise 2.
   - Underline the key words in their counter-arguments and rebuttals.
   - Swap their answers with a partner to get feedback.
   - Give feedback to their partner answering the question:
     - *Does the rebuttal directly attack the key point in the counter-argument?*
2. Elicit answers.

Option 2

1. Have students:
   - Swap textbooks with a partner.
   - Write a rebuttal to their partner's counter-arguments in Exercise 2.
2. Then have students:
   - Return the textbooks.
   - Read their partner's rebuttal and underline the key words in them.
   - Give feedback to their partner answering the question:
     - *Does the rebuttal directly attack the key point in the counter-argument?*
3. Elicit answers.

| Section 4 | Organizing an argumentative essay |

Option 1

1. Have students draw the following table:

Framework A		Framework B
Introduction		Introduction
Body paragraph 1		Body paragraph 1
Body paragraph 2		Body paragraph 2
Body paragraph 3		Body paragraph 3
Conclusion		Conclusion

2. Then have students:
   - Look at the organizational frameworks in the textbook for one minute.
   - Close their textbooks and complete the table (individually or in pairs).
   - Compare what they have written with the information in the textbook.
3. Elicit answers. (Answer: See table, page 64)

Option 2

1. Have students read the explanation.
2. Have students, in pairs or small groups and with books closed, recall what they read.
3. Elicit:
   - *What are the two possible frameworks of an argumentative essay?*
4. As students give answers correctly, draw the two frameworks on the board. (Answer: See table, page 64)
5. Re-emphasize:
   - *In Framework A, counter-arguments are presented in the third body paragraph only.*
   - *In Framework B, there must be a specific counter-argument to the main idea in each paragraph.*

Exercise 5

Option 1

1. Have students complete the exercise individually.

2. Then have students compare answers with a partner.

3. Elicit answers.

Option 2

1. Have students read the essay and complete items 1 and 2 individually.

2. Then in pairs, have students:
   - Summarize the essay to each other.
   - Compare their answers to items 1 and 2.
   - Do item 3 collaboratively without looking back at the essay.

3. Elicit answers.

Option 3

1. Follow Option 1 or 2 above.

2. Then have students:
   - Underline the expressions that are used to introduce the counter-arguments in the body paragraphs.
   - Underline the expressions that introduce the rebuttals.

3. Elicit:
   - *What expressions were used to introduce the counter-arguments?* (Answer: **Body paragraph 2 – "Those who . . . may argue . . .," "Another objection . . . may be . . ."**)
   - *What expressions were used to introduce the rebuttals?* (Answer: **"However, . . .," "While this is true . . ."**)

4. Emphasize:
   - *These are very useful expressions when writing counter-arguments and rebuttals.*

5. Have students underline the in-text citation in the rebuttals. [Answer: **(Johnson and Swinton 110), (Wagner 128), (Horthorn 52)**]

6. Emphasize:
   - It is important to use outside evidence in rebuttals.

Option 4

1. Follow Option 1, 2, or 3 above.

2. Divide the class into small groups.

3. Have the groups discuss:
   - *Do you agree with the writer's position?*

4. Elicit answers.

Exercise 6

Option 1

1. Have students complete the exercise individually.

2. Have students compare answers with a partner.

3. Elicit answers.

Option 2

1. Have students read the essay individually.

2. Then in pairs, have students:
   - Summarize the essay to each other.

- Do the outline collaboratively without looking back at the essay.

3. Elicit answers.

Option 3

1. Follow Option 1 or 2 above.

2. Then have students:
   - Underline the expressions that are used to introduce the counter-arguments in the body paragraphs.
   - Underline the expressions that introduce the rebuttals.
   - Underline the in-text citation in the rebuttals.

3. Elicit:
   - *What expressions were used to introduce the counter-arguments?* (Answer: **Body paragraph 1 – "Some people may argue . . ."; body paragraph 2 – "While those . . . may insist . . ."**)
   - *What expressions were used to introduce the rebuttals?* (Answer: **Body paragraph 1 – "However, . . ."; Body paragraph 2 – "this may not always be true"**)
   - *How were the rebuttals cited?* [Answer: **Body paragraph 1 – (Horthorn 52); body paragraph 2 – (Jordin 40)**]

Option 4

1. After completing the outline, in pairs or small groups, have students:
   - Brainstorm ideas for body paragraph 3 based on the topic sentence (at the bottom of page 68).
   - Add to the outline at the bottom of page 69 with information on body paragraph 3.
   - Swap the outline with another pair/group to compare.

2. Elicit answers.

Option for both Exercises 5 and 6

1. Divide the class into pairs.

2. Have one student in each pair complete Exercise 5. Have the other student complete Exercise 6.

3. In addition, have students:
   - Underline the expressions used to introduce the counter-arguments.
   - Underline the expressions used to introduce the rebuttals.

4. Then with their partner, have students discuss:
   - *How were the two different essays organized?*
   - *What expressions were used to introduce the counter-arguments and rebuttals?*

5. Elicit answers.

UNIT 3

Part 2
Organizing argumentative essays

Introductory paragraph of an argumentative essay

1. In pairs or small groups, have students discuss:
    *   *What are the three parts of an introductory paragraph?*
    *   *What is the function of each part?*

Note: The preceding questions are a review of Unit 1 Part 1, Section 2.

2. Elicit answers.
    (Answer)
    *   **Hook – introduces the topic of the essay in an interesting way**
    *   **Building sentences – provide background on the topic and help the reader to understand the thesis**
    *   **Thesis statement – states the topic, writer's position, and main ideas**

1. Direct and indirect thesis statements

Option 1

1. Have students read the explanation.
2. Elicit:
    *   *What is the difference between a direct and an indirect thesis statement?* (Answer: **A direct thesis lists the main ideas; an indirect thesis statement summarizes the main ideas.**)
    *   *When can a direct thesis statement be used?* (Answer: **For a short essay that only has two or three main ideas**)
    *   *If an indirect thesis statement is used, where should the main ideas be introduced?* (Answer: **In the building sentences**)
3. Emphasize:
    *   *Although indirect thesis statements must be used in longer essays, they can also be used in shorter essays.*
4. Have students read the example introductory paragraphs on page 71.

Option 2

1. To review thesis statements, write the following question on the board:
    *   *Wearing school uniforms should be compulsory for all high school students. Do you agree or disagree with this statement?*
2. Have students discuss the question in pairs or small groups.
3. Find out the majority opinion from the class by getting a show of hands. Ask:
    *   *Do you agree with this statement? Hands up.* (Count the hands.)
    *   *Do you disagree with this statement? Hands up.* (Count the hands.)

4. Write the majority opinion on the board:
    High school students should be required to wear uniforms.
    OR
    High school students should not be required to wear uniforms.
5. Elicit reasons to support the majority opinion. (Possible answers)
    *   For: **They save students' time, they develop a school identity, they make it easy to identify intruders**
        OR
    *   Against: **They reduce students' freedom of expression, they are ugly, they are an unnecessary expense**
6. Add the reasons that support the majority opinion to the answer on the board. (Possible answer: **High school students should be required to wear uniforms as they save students' time, they develop a school identity, and they make it easy to identify intruders.**)
7. Explain:
    *   *This is a direct thesis statement. It contains a topic, thesis, and main ideas.*
    *   *It is appropriate for a short essay because there are only three main ideas that can be easily written in a one-sentence thesis statement.*
8. Elicit:
    *   *Would a direct thesis statement be appropriate for a long essay that has five main ideas?* (Answer: **No. The thesis statement would be too long. In this situation, an indirect thesis statement would be appropriate.**)
9. Write an example of an indirect thesis statement by crossing out the main ideas in the direct thesis statement on the board. (Possible answer: **High school students should be required to wear uniforms as they** ~~save students' time, they develop a school identity, and they make it easy to identify intruders.~~ **benefit both the students and the schools in a number of ways.**)
10. Explain:
    *   *In an indirect thesis statement, the topic and position are still given, but only a summary of the main ideas is written.*
    *   *The main ideas themselves must be introduced in the building sentences. If they are not introduced, the reader will not be able to understand the direction of the essay.*
11. Emphasize:
    *   *Although indirect thesis statements must be used in longer essays, they can also be used in shorter essays, if the writer chooses to do so.*

12. Have students read the example introductory paragraphs (page 71).

2. Introducing a counter-argument

1. To review counter-arguments, elicit from students:
   - *What are the two frameworks for including counter-arguments in the body of an argumentative essay?* (Answer: See diagram, page 64)

2. Then have students read the explanation at the top of page 72.

3. Elicit:
   - *Where should the counter-arguments be introduced?* (Answer: **In the introductory paragraph; before the thesis statement**)

4. Have students read the example.

Exercise 1

Option 1

1. Have students complete the exercise individually.

2. Then have students compare answers with a partner.

3. Elicit answers.

Option 2

1. Follow Option 1 above.

2. Then have students:
   - Underline the phrase that introduces the counter-argument.
   - Look back at the model essay on page 65 and underline the phrase in the introductory paragraph that introduces the counter-argument.

3. Elicit answers. (Answer: **page 73 – "Some, however, claim . . ."; page 65 – "Some people believe that . . ."**)

4. Emphasize:
   - *These are very common phrases when introducing a counter-argument.*

Exercise 2

Option 1

1. Have students work individually to complete the exercise.

2. Emphasize:
   - *It is only necessary to add the main ideas to the building sentences, and modify the thesis statement so that it effectively summarizes the main ideas.*

3. Have students compare their introductory paragraph with a partner.

4. Elicit answers.

Option 2

1. Divide the class into pairs.

2. Have students work collaboratively to complete the exercise.

3. Emphasize:
   - *It is only necessary to add the main ideas to the building sentences, and modify the thesis statement so that it effectively summarizes the main ideas.*

4. Have pairs compare their introductory paragraph with another pair.

5. Elicit answers.

Section 2 — Body paragraphs of an argumentative essay

1. To review the organization of body paragraphs, elicit:
   - *What are the five sentence types in body paragraphs?* (Answer: **Topic sentence, a sentence giving a reason, a sentence giving evidence, a sentence giving explanation, concluding sentence**)

2. Have students read the explanation.

1. Phrases to introduce an argument

Option 1

1. Write the following sentences on the board:
   I think that studying English increases employment opportunities.
   I believe that university education plays a key role in preparing young people for employment.

2. Elicit:
   - *Why are these sentences not appropriate in an academic essay?* (Answer: **They are too personal. *I* should not be used.**)

3. Have students read the phrases in the textbook.

4. Then have students rewrite the sentences on the board using two different phrases.

5. Elicit answers.

6. Emphasize:
   - *The choice of phrase indicates how strongly the writer believes the argument (e.g., "There is no doubt . . ." is much stronger than "There is evidence to suggest that . . .").*

Option 2

1. Follow Option 1 above.

2. Then choose one of the following two topics for discussion and write it on the board:
   - *Whether or not to abolish the death penalty*
   - *The most appropriate age at which to start studying a second language*

3. In pairs or small groups, have students discuss:
   - *What is your position on this topic?*
   - *What arguments support your position?*

4. Instruct students:
   - *Use the phrases on page 74 in your discussions.*

5. Select a few pairs/groups and elicit their answers.

Exercise 3

1. Have students complete the exercise individually.
2. Then have students compare answers with a partner.
3. Elicit answers.

Exercise 4

1. Have students complete the exercise individually.
2. Instruct students:
   - *Use a phrase that accurately reflects how strongly you personally believe the argument.*
3. Have students compare answers with a partner.
4. Elicit answers.

2. Transitional expressions

Option 1

1. Elicit:
   - *What does cohesion mean?* (Answer: **Sticking together; in academic writing this means having a logical flow**)
   - *How can writers make their essays cohesive?* (Answer: **By clearly showing the relationship between ideas; this can be done by using transitional expressions**)
2. Draw the following table on the board:

Function	Transitional expressions
To list ideas	First,
To add an idea	Also,
To introduce a contrasting idea	However,
To show an example	For example,
To show an effect or result	Therefore,
To give an alternative consequence	Otherwise,
To restate an idea given in the previous sentence	In other words,

3. In pairs or small groups, have students brainstorm ideas for each part of the table.
4. Elicit answers and complete the table as correct answers are given.
5. Have students compare the table on the board with the one in the textbook.

Option 2

1. Have students read the explanation.
2. Elicit:
   - *What is a transitional expression?* (Answer: **Words/phrases that show a relationship between ideas**)

- *What does cohesion mean?* (Answer: **Sticking together; in academic writing this means having a logical flow**)
- *What punctuation usually follows a transitional expression?* (Answer: **A comma**)
3. Instruct students to refer to this table when they are writing their own essays, and to use a number of different expressions to vary their writing style.

Option 3

1. Divide students into pairs (Student A and Student B).
2. Have all the students read and memorize the first and second columns of the table.
3. Then have:
   - All of the Student As close their books.
   - Student Bs test Student As by asking:
     - *What transitional expression is used to . . . (list ideas, add an idea, etc.)?*

Exercise 5

Option 1

1. Have students complete the exercise individually.
2. Then have students compare answers with a partner.
3. Elicit answers.

Option 2

1. Follow Option 1 above.
2. Then have each student:
   - Write three examples of sentence pairs that are missing a transitional expression.
   - Swap their examples with a partner.
   - Write in an appropriate transitional expression for each of their partner's sentence pairs.
3. Have students check each other's work.
4. Elicit a few sample sentence pairs with transitional expressions.

3. Improving paragraph-to-paragraph cohesion

1. Explain:
   - *It is not only important to have cohesion within paragraphs, it is also important to have cohesion between paragraphs.*
2. Have students read the explanation.
3. Emphasize:
   - *Transitional words, or phrases, or a mixture of both, are an easy way to achieve paragraph-to-paragraph cohesion.*

Exercise 6

1. Have students complete the exercise individually.
2. Emphasize:
   - *More than one answer is possible for a number of the blanks.*
3. Have students compare answers with a partner.
4. Elicit answers.

4. Support from outside sources

1. Draw the following table on the board (explain that it represents a body paragraph):

Topic sentence
Reason
Explanation
Reason
Explanation
Concluding sentence

2. Elicit:
   - *What is missing?* (Answer: **The evidence**)

3. Then elicit:
   - *What different types of information can be used as evidence?* (Answer: **Authoritative opinions, specific examples, statistical evidence**)

4. Have students read the examples of each type of information.

5. Emphasize:
   - *Without information citing outside sources, readers have little reason to trust what you say because they do not know you.*
   - *Including cited information shows that the ideas being expressed are not just your own, but are supported by other, more respected people or research.*

5. Concluding sentences in body paragraphs

Option 1

1. Elicit:
   - *What is the function of a concluding sentence?* (Answer: **To summarize the reasons in the paragraph and show their relevance to the writer's position**)

2. Have students read the first (poor) example paragraph.

3. Emphasize:
   - *The lack of an explanation of the relevance of the evidence makes the writer's argument very hard to understand.*
   - *It is the writer's responsibility to explain the connections between the reasons in the body paragraph and the position in the thesis statement. The reader should not have to work to try to understand what the writer is saying.*
   - *Therefore, a paragraph must not finish with information from outside sources because, after providing such information, the writer must always explain its relevance.*

4. Have students read the second (good) example paragraph.

5. Emphasize:
   - *In the second example paragraph, it is clearer to the reader how the points in the paragraph support the thesis.*

- *Therefore, this style of writing is much more likely to convince the reader of the strength of a writer's position.*

Option 2

1. Have students read the first example paragraph.

2. Elicit:
   - *What is the reason or claim made in the first sentence?* (Answer: **Wikipedia's value = breadth of information**)

3. When the right answer is given, write it on the board.

4. Then elicit:
   - *What evidence is given to support this claim?* (Answer: **3.5 million entries, hyperlinks, multilingual**)

5. List the correct answers on the board as they are given.

6. Then elicit:
   - *What was the position in the thesis of this essay?* (Answer: **See textbook page 57: Wikipedia provides a useful starting point for research**)

7. When the right answer is given, write it on the board.

8. Then elicit:
   - *How is all of this evidence related to the position in the thesis?*

9. Elicit a few answers.

10. Then have students look at the last two sentences of the second example paragraph.

11. Elicit:
    - *How does the writer explain the relationship between the evidence and the thesis?* (Answer)
      - **The writer explains that Wikipedia is a "'one-stop resource' for research."**
      - **Then the writer follows up by emphasizing that Wikipedia has "democratized knowledge" thanks to the large amount of information that can be accessed and edited by anyone, which is essential for research.**

Section 3 | The concluding paragraph of an argumentative essay

Option 1

To review the points in Unit 1 Part 2 on the concluding paragraph:

1. Write *Concluding paragraph* on the board.

2. Then elicit:
   - *What are the three parts of a concluding paragraph?* (Answer: **Restated thesis, summary of main points, final thought**)

3. As correct answers are given, list them on the board.

4. Elicit:
   - *When restating the thesis statement, what should be omitted and what should be changed?*
   (Answer)
     - **The main ideas should be omitted, so as to avoid repetition in the concluding paragraph.**
     - **The vocabulary and the structure should be changed.**
   - *What different types of final thought can be used?* (Answer: **Opinion or judgment, solution or recommendation, prediction or speculation**)
   - *What should the final thought not do?* (Answer: **It should not introduce a new idea.**)
5. Have students read the example concluding paragraph.
6. Elicit:
   - *What type of final thought is presented in the paragraph?* (Answer: **Opinion**)

Option 2

1. Have students read the explanation and example concluding paragraph.
2. In pairs, have students discuss:
   - *Why is this an effective concluding paragraph?*
3. Elicit answers.
   (Answers)
   - **It has a restated thesis that uses different vocabulary and structure than the original.**
   - **It has a summary of the main points that explains the main ideas and what can be concluded about each.**
   - **It has a final thought that gives an opinion on what the achievements of Wikipedia show.**
4. Emphasize:
   - *An argumentative essay's concluding paragraph has the same three parts as an expository essay's concluding paragraph.*

Section 1 Avoiding overgeneralization

1. Write the following sentences on the board:
   - *Japanese people enjoy eating raw fish.*
   - *People believe that economic development is harmful to the environment.*
   - *Children learn second languages more quickly than adults.*

2. Elicit:
   - *What is the problem with these sentences?* (Answer: **They are overgeneralizations, because they are not true in 100 percent of cases. This makes it appear that the writer has not considered the issue carefully.**)

3. Emphasize:
   - *Writers can avoid overgeneralizations by hedging.*

4. Have students read the explanation and hedging expressions.

5. Have students work in pairs to rewrite the three sentences above.
   (Possible answers)
   - **Many Japanese people enjoy eating raw fish.**
   - **Some people believe that economic development may be harmful to the environment.**
   - **Research indicates that children tend learn second languages more quickly than adults.**

6. Emphasize:
   - *Overgeneralization is a common problem in essays. Students need to be aware of the potential danger of doing this.*
   - *Overgeneralizations make it seem that the writer is uninformed, unaware that the statement is not true, or presenting ideas without thinking deeply about them. This could have a negative impact on the reader, who might begin to doubt the writer's views and/or writing ability.*
   - *An overgeneralization may also potentially upset some readers who take offense to stereotyping of certain types of people or subjects.*

Exercise 1

Option 1

1. Have students complete the exercise individually.

2. Then have students compare answers with a partner.

3. Elicit answers.

4. Emphasize:
   - *Hedging language is often used in academic writing.*
   - *If a claim is not 100 percent true, then hedge it.*

Option 2

1. Follow Option 1 above.

2. Have students:
   - Write three overgeneralizations.
   - Swap their overgeneralizations with a partner.
   - Rewrite the sentences using hedging language.

3. Elicit sentences and rewrites.

Section 2 Avoiding redundancy

1. Have students read only the explanation at the bottom of page 83.

2. Write the following sentences from the textbook on the board:
   - *The basic fundamentals of successful language learning are motivation and practice.*
   - *If students do not understand, the teacher will repeat the question again.*
   - *One benefit of studying abroad is that one can experience a country's language and culture directly. People are more exposed to the language and culture by living in the country.*

3. Elicit: *What is the problem with these sentences?* (Answer: **They repeat information unnecessarily.**) Explain that this is called "redundancy."

4. Have students rewrite the examples.

5. Then have students read the rest of the explanation in the textbook and compare their answers with the examples.

Exercise 2

Option 1

1. Have students complete the exercise individually.

2. Then have students compare answers with a partner.

3. Elicit answers.

Option 2

1. Divide the class into pairs.

2. Have students work collaboratively to complete the exercise.

3. Elicit answers.

Note:
   - Identifying redundant sentences is particularly challenging for students because they often

think a redundant sentence is giving a further explanation or emphasizing a point.

- Therefore, having students work together on this type of activity gives them a better chance to find redundancies.

Option 3

Explain: *Finding redundancies can be challenging. Some reasons are:*

1. *A redundant word may be perceived as an "intensifier" – a way to emphasize something, for example:*
   - **He was the top champion in his sport.**
     "Top" and "champion" have essentially the same meaning, so this is redundant. However, an intensifier modifies the level of the subject, for example:
   - **He was the most respected champion in his sport.**
     There were likely other champions in this person's sport, but there was something noteworthy about this particular champion – "most respected."

2. *A redundant sentence may be perceived as a further explanation of the sentence before it, for example (from the book):*
   - **One benefit of studying abroad is that one can experience a country's language and culture directly. People are more exposed to the language and culture by living in the country.**
     The second sentence has the same meaning as the sentence before. It does not provide any further insight on the subject. Any further explanation on the subject should help readers have a deeper understanding of the subject, for example:
   - **One benefit of studying abroad is that one can experience a country's language and culture directly. This often leads to people learning a language quicker thanks to increased exposure and motivation.**
     The second sentence explains what directly experiencing a country's language and culture can lead to.

Section 3 | Avoiding vague or "empty" words

Option 1

1. Write the following sentences from the textbook on the board:
   English is an important language in the world.
   The linguist Barry McLaughlin is a widely respected person.
   The experience of learning English can often be difficult and time-consuming.

2. Elicit: *Why are these sentences not effective?* (Answer: **They contain vague words without a precise meaning**.)

3. Have students work in small groups to rewrite the sentences.

4. Then have students read the explanation and compare their answers with the examples in the textbook.

5. Emphasize:
   - *If making a claim, such as something is "important," "interesting," "different," or "challenging," give a reason to support that claim, either in the same sentence or in the following sentences.*
   - *Otherwise be more specific in your description. Do NOT make the reader guess what you mean.*

Exercise 3

Option 1

1. Have students complete the exercise individually.

2. Then have students compare answers with a partner.

3. Elicit answers.

Option 2

1. Divide the class into pairs.

2. Have students work collaboratively to complete the exercise.

3. Elicit answers.

Note:
- Identifying vague or empty words is particularly challenging for students because there is nothing grammatically wrong with the sentences.
- Therefore, having students work together on this type of activity gives them a better chance of finding such types of words.

Section 4 | Revising an argumentative essay

Option 1

1. Have students read the checklist.

2. Encourage students to clarify the meaning of any of the items with a partner or the teacher. This is a good opportunity to review the material that has been covered.

3. Explain to students that some of these questions may be easier to answer when looking at their own essay, and some of them may be easier when looking at another person's essay.

Option 2

1. Have students read the explanation and first draft checklist in the textbook.

2. As students are reading, write the following on the board:
   First draft checklist:
   - *Whole essay*
   - *Introductory paragraph*
   - *Body paragraphs*
   - *Counter-arguments and rebuttals*
   - *Concluding paragraph*
   - *Language and coherence*

3. Then have students, in pairs or small groups and with books closed, recall what they read.

4. Elicit answers to the following:
   - *What are questions you can ask about the whole essay?*
   - *What are questions you can ask about the introductory paragraph?*
   - *What are questions you can ask about the body paragraphs?*
   - *What are questions you can ask about counter-arguments and rebuttals?*
   - *What are questions you can ask about the concluding paragraph?*
   - *What are questions you can ask about language and coherence?*

   (Answers: See textbook page 86, checklist)

Exercise 4

Option 1

1. Have students read the draft.
2. Then have students individually revise the draft using the checklist.
3. Divide the class into pairs or small groups.
4. Have students compare the revisions that they have made. Remind students to focus not just on explaining weaknesses, but also on explaining why some parts of the essay are good.
5. Elicit answers.

Option 2

1. Have students read the draft.
2. Divide the class into pairs or small groups.
3. Have the pairs/groups work collaboratively to revise the draft using the checklist.
4. Then have each pair/group swap their revised draft with another pair/group to compare the revisions they have made.
5. Elicit answers.

Option 3

1. Follow Option 1 or 2 above.
2. Then, in pairs or small groups, have students discuss whether or not they agree with the writer's position.

UNIT 4

Part 1
Compare and contrast essay structure

Starting a compare and contrast essay

1. Have students read the explanation.
2. Elicit:
   - *What are the goals of a compare and contrast essay?*
     (Answer)
     - **To gain a deeper understanding of the subjects being compared**
     - **To either explain the similarities/differences of the subjects in detail, or to make an argument about the similarities/differences of the subjects**
   - *What steps should you follow before writing a compare and contrast essay?* (Answer: See list in the middle of page 90)

   Note: Terms such as *a reason for comparison* and *points of comparison* will be explained in detail later in the unit.

1. Establish a reason for comparison

Option 1

1. Have students read the explanation.
2. Elicit:
   - *Why must a compare and contrast essay have a reason for comparison?* (Answer: **It gives the essay a focus and helps to guide the research.**)
3. Emphasize:
   - *All essays need a motive. For compare and contrast essay, this is called "a reason for comparison."*
   - *Some essay questions provide a reason for comparison; some do not.*
   - *If there is no reason given, the writer must consider a reason.*

Option 2

1. Write the following essay questions from the textbook on the board:
   Compare and contrast how students are educated in public and home schools.
   Compare and contrast public and private schools in your country.
2. In pairs or small groups, have students discuss:
   - *Which question would likely be easier to write about?*
   - *What is the potential problem with the second question?*
3. Elicit answers.
   (Answers)
   - **The first question would be easier to write about because it has a focus, a "reason for comparison" that can help give guidance to a writer.**

   - **There are so many things to write about regarding the two subjects. The writer risks just choosing random points of comparison and writing an unfocused essay.**
4. Elicit:
   - *What should writers do to solve the problem with the second question?* (Answer: **They need to consider a reason for comparison – something that makes it clear to readers what the value is of comparing the two subjects.**)
5. In pairs or small groups, have students discuss:
   - *What are potential reasons for comparison between the two subjects in question 2? (Compare and contrast public and private schools in your country.)*
6. Elicit answers. (Answers: **The difficulty of academics and courses, the students who attend, the resources provided**)

Exercise 1

Option 1

1. Have students work in pairs to complete the exercise.
2. Elicit answers.

Option 2

1. Have students complete the exercise individually.
2. Then have students compare answers with a partner.
3. Elicit answers.

2. Choose points of comparison

Option 1

1. Have students read the explanation.
2. Explain:
   - *Points of comparison are areas where the two subjects can be directly compared.*
3. Divide the class into pairs or small groups.
4. Have groups brainstorm points of comparison that could be used to compare the USA and the UK.
5. Elicit some of the ideas and write them on the board. (Possible answers: **Size, population, language spoken, food eaten, cultural diversity, history, main religions**)
6. Emphasize:
   - *These aspects are rather random, so if you simply wrote an essay comparing the USA and the UK, the essay would have no focus.*
   - *Therefore, a reason to compare them is needed.*

7. Elicit:
   - *If the essay question was "Compare the USA and the UK. Which country is easier for new immigrants to adjust to?", which of the aspects would be relevant?* (Possible answers: **Food, language spoken, cultural diversity**)
   (**Note:** This essay question will be referred to again in Sections 3 and 4.)

8. Emphasize:
   - *When writing a compare and contrast essay, the points of comparison must be relevant to the reason for comparison.*
   - *If they are not, they should not be included in the essay.*
   - *Therefore, in the essay above, a point such as "the size of the country" would probably not be included.*

Option 2

1. Write the following question from the textbook on the board:
   Compare and contrast how students are educated in public and home schools.

2. Elicit:
   - *What is the reason for comparison?* (Answer: **How students are educated**)

3. Then in pairs or groups, have students discuss:
   - *What points are related to how students are educated in school?*

4. Elicit answers. (Possible answers: **Curriculum, teachers, other students, materials, resources, homework, time spent in class**)

5. Have students read the explanation in the textbook.

Exercise 2

Option 1

1. Have students complete the exercise individually or in pairs.

2. Then have students compare answers with a partner or another pair.

3. Instruct students to give feedback based on the question:
   - *Are all of the points of comparison closely related to the reason for comparison?*

4. Elicit answers.

Option 2

1. Have students work in pairs to brainstorm reasons for comparison only.

2. Have pairs swap textbooks with another pair, and then brainstorm points of comparison based on the reasons for comparison that the other pair chose.

3. When done, have students return textbooks to the original pair to compare ideas.

3. Writing a thesis statement
Option 1

To review thesis statements in general, elicit:
1. *What is the purpose of a thesis statement?* (Answer: **To tell the reader what the essay is about and what will be included in the body of the essay**)

2. *Where should it be located?* (Answer: **The final sentence of the introductory paragraph**)

3. *How long should it be?* (Answer: **One sentence**)

Option 2

1. Have students read the explanation.

2. Elicit:
   - *What should a thesis statement in a compare and contrast essay contain?*
   (Answer)
     - **The two subjects being compared/contrasted**
     - **Their relationship (similar/different/both)**
     - **The reason for comparison**
     - **The points of comparison**

3. Emphasize:
   - *The thesis statement is the most important sentence in the essay, as it is the answer to the question.*

Option 3

1. Follow Option 2 above.

2. Write the question from Section 2, "Choose points of comparison," Option 1 on the board:
   Compare the USA and the UK. Which country is easier for new immigrants to adjust to?

3. Under the question write the three possible points of comparison:
   food, language spoken, cultural diversity

4. In pairs or small groups, have students write a thesis statement.

5. Elicit answers.
   (Possible answer)
   - **As a result of the languages spoken, the food eaten, and the levels of cultural diversity, both the USA and the UK are relatively simple countries for new immigrants to acclimatize to.**

Option 4

1. Have students read the explanation.

2. With books closed, elicit:
   - *What are the 4 elements of a compare and contrast essay thesis statement?* [Answer: **The two subjects being compared/contrasted; their relationship (similar/different/both); the reason for comparison; the points of comparison**]

3. Relate this information about thesis statements to what students have studied earlier in the book about thesis statements. Emphasize:
   - *"The two subjects" are like the "topic."*
   - *"Their relationship" and the "reason for comparison" are like the "writer's position."*
   - *The "points of comparison" are like the "main ideas."*

Exercise 3

Option 1

1. Divide the class into pairs.

2. Have each pair write a thesis statement for item 1.

3. Elicit answers and write them on the board.

4. In each thesis statement, identify the essential parts (the two subjects, the relationship, the reason for comparison, the points of comparison).

5. If any of the essential parts are missing, elicit how to improve the thesis statement.

6. Have students complete items 2 and 3 individually.

7. Then have students swap with a partner.

8. Have the partner identify the essential parts of each thesis statement (the two subjects, the relationship, the reason for comparison, the points of comparison).

9. Then have students give feedback to their partner.

10. Elicit answers.

Option 2

1. Have students work individually to write thesis statements. (**Note:** Some students may find this challenging. Be prepared to assist weaker students.)

2. Have students swap their thesis statements with a partner.

3. Have the partner identify the essential parts of each thesis statement (the two subjects, the relationship, the reason for comparison, the points of comparison).

4. Then have students give feedback to their partner.

5. Elicit answers.

4. Select an essay pattern

Option 1

To review essay organization:
1. Draw the following table on the board:

Introductory paragraph
Body paragraphs
Concluding paragraph

2. Elicit:
    - *What are the three parts of an introductory paragraph?* (Answer: **Hook, building sentences, thesis**)
    - *What are the three parts of a body paragraphs?* (Answer: **Topic sentence, supporting sentences, concluding sentence**)
    - *What are the three parts of a concluding paragraph?* (Answer: **Restated thesis, summary of the main ideas, final thought**)

Option 2

1. Follow Option 1 above.

2. Then have students read the explanation for both compare and contrast essay patterns on pages 95 and 96.

3. In pairs or small groups, have students discuss:
    - *What is the difference between the two patterns?*

4. Elicit answers.
    (Answer)
    - subject by subject:
      - **There are two body paragraphs.**
      - **The points of comparison for one subject are presented in the first body paragraph.**
      - **Similar points of comparison are presented in the second body paragraph in the same order as the first.**
      - **More appropriate for shorter essays.**
    - point by point:
      1. **One body paragraph for each point of comparison between the two subjects.**
      2. **Can be used for shorter or longer essays.**

Option 3

1. Follow Option 2 above.

2. Then have students focus on the Pattern 1 table (page 95) and the Pattern 2 table (page 96).

3. In pairs or small groups, have students draw similar tables for the "Compare the USA and the UK. Which country is easier for new immigrants to adjust to?" essay question from the previous section.

4. Elicit answers and draw them on the board.
    (Answers)
    Pattern 1: subject by subject

1. Introductory paragraph
2. Body paragraph 1: The USA
A. Languages spoken
B. Food eaten
C. Levels of cultural diversity
3. Body paragraph 2: The UK
A. Languages spoken
B. Food eaten
C. Levels of cultural diversity
4. Concluding paragraph

Pattern 2: point by point

1. Introductory paragraph
2. Body paragraph 1: Languages spoken   **Similarities and/or differences between the USA and the UK**
3. Body paragraph 2: Food eaten   **Similarities and/or differences between the USA and the UK**
4. Body paragraph 3: Level of cultural diversity   **Similarities and/or differences between the USA and the UK**
5. Concluding paragraph

5. Emphasize:
   - *If using a subject by subject pattern of organization, the points of comparison must be organized in the same order in each body paragraph.*
   - *If using a subject by subject pattern, there will only be two body paragraphs. If using a point by point pattern, there will be three body paragraphs (or one for each point of comparison).*

Exercise 4

Option 1

1. Have students complete the exercise individually.
2. Have students compare answers with a partner.
3. Elicit answers.

Option 2

1. Follow Option 1 above.
2. Divide the class into small groups.
3. Have students discuss:
   - *Do you think home schools and public schools provide the same level of education?*
4. Elicit answers.

5. Outline the essay

To review the importance of outlining an essay:
1. Elicit:
   - *Why is it important to make an essay outline?* (Answer: **In order to write a well-organized essay**)
   - *What information should be included in an outline?* (Answer: **The thesis statement, topic sentences, main ideas, and the supporting details that will be used in the essay**)
2. Have students read the explanation.

Exercise 5

Option 1

1. Have students complete the exercise individually.
2. Then, in pairs or small groups, have students compare their answers.

3. As students are comparing their answers, draw the following table on the board:

Point of Comparison	Subject 1	Subject 2

4. Elicit points of comparison and details. Fill in the table on the board.
5. When done with one pair of subjects, erase the contents of the table.
6. For the next pair of subjects, repeat from step 4.

Option 2

1. Divide the class into pairs or small groups.
2. Have one member of each pair/group create an outline for one of the topics.
3. When done, within their pair or group, have students explain their outlines to each other.

UNIT 4

Part 2
Describing similarities and differences

Section 1 **Words and phrases to describe similarities and differences**

Option 1

1. Have students read the explanation.

2. Emphasize:
   In a compare and contrast essay, it is essential to accurately use specific vocabulary to express similarities and differences.

Option 2

1. Write the following sentences on the board:
   Dogs are very attentive. However, cats are more independent.
   Dogs bark. However, cats meow.
   Dogs need to be walked. However, cats do not.

2. Elicit: *What is wrong with this set of sentences?* (Answer: **"However" is overused; more variety is needed to keep from repeating the same words, which is bad writing style.**)

3. Emphasize:
   * *It is important to use a variety of words in order to reduce repetition.*

Exercise 1

Option 1

1. Divide the class into pairs.

2. Have students work collaboratively to complete the exercise.

3. Elicit answers.

Option 2

1. Divide the class into pairs (Student A and Student B).

2. Have:
   * Student A brainstorm words for describing similarities.
   * Student B brainstorm words for expressing differences.

3. Have students share their lists with each other and suggest additional words/phrases.

4. Elicit answers.

5. Then have:
   * Student A read the sample essays to find words that express similarities.
   * Student B read the sample essays to find words that express differences.

6. Have students show each other the parts they underlined.

7. Elicit answers.

Describing similarities
Option 1

1. Have students read the explanation and information in the table.

2. In pairs or small groups, have students try to recall as much of the information as they can.

3. Elicit answers.

Option 2

1. Have students read the explanation and information in the table.

2. Explain that it is not necessary to memorize all this vocabulary, but students should use this page as a guide when they start to write their own essays.

Exercise 2

Option 1

1. Have students complete the exercise individually.

2. Then have students compare answers with a partner.

3. Elicit answers.

Option 2

1. Follow Option 1 above.

2. Have each student write three sentences that explain a similarity between two subjects, but omit the words/phrases that express the similarity.

3. Then have students:
   * Swap their sentences with a partner.
   * Complete the sentences of their partner.

Describing differences
Option 1

1. Have students read the explanation and information in the table.

2. In pairs or small groups, have students try to recall as much of the information as they can.

3. Elicit answers.

Option 2

1. Have students read the explanation and information in the table.

2. Explain that it is not necessary to memorize all this vocabulary, but students should use this page as a guide when they start to write their own essays.

Exercise 3

Option 1

1. Have students complete the exercise individually.
2. Then have students compare answers with a partner.
3. Elicit answers.

Option 2

1. Follow Option 1 above.
2. Have each student write three sentences that explain a difference between two subjects, but omit the words/phrases that express the difference.
3. Then have students:
   - Swap their sentences with a partner.
   - Complete the sentences of their partner.

Exercise 4

Option 1

1. Have students complete the exercise individually.
2. Then have students compare answers with a partner.
3. Elicit answers.

Option 2

1. Divide the class into pairs.
2. Have students work collaboratively to complete the exercise.
3. Elicit answers.

Section 2 Parallel structure

Option 1

1. Have students read the explanation.
2. Elicit:
   - *What is a "parallel structure"?* (Answer: **Using the same grammatical structure**)
   - *Why is it useful when listing ideas?* (Answer: **It often makes sentences clear and natural in style.**)
3. Emphasize:
   - *While the poor examples in the textbook are not grammatically incorrect, they are unnatural.*

Option 2

1. Write the poor example sentences from the textbook on the board:
   In single sex schools, boys often have fewer chances to study home economics, practice cheerleading, and they do not take dance classes. Alternative schools offer students closer relationships with their teacher, more choice over which subjects to study, and the class sizes are small.
2. Elicit:
   - *What is wrong with these sentences?* (Answer: **The last point in each sentence lacks parallel structure with the other two points.**)
   - *How can these sentences be fixed?* (Answers)
     Sentence 1: "they do not take" → **take**
     Sentence 2: "the class sizes are small" → **smaller class sizes than public schools**
3. Have students read the explanation in the textbook about how to fix these sentences.

UNIT 4

Part 3
Improving your work

Section 1 — Using commas

1. Write the following sentences from the textbook on the board:

   Although they are happy to work in groups boys often prefer to work individually.

   Boys whether in same-sex or co-educational schools often prefer to work individually.

   Boys often prefer to work individually but they are also happy to work in groups.

2. Elicit:
   • *Where should a comma be added in each sentence?*

3. Insert commas in the sentences on the board as the students suggest.

4. Then have students read the explanation and compare the sentences on the board with those in the textbook.

Exercise 1

Option 1

1. Have students complete the exercise individually.

2. Then have students compare answers with a partner.

3. Elicit answers.

Option 2

1. Divide the class into pairs

2. Have students work collaboratively to complete the exercise.

3. Elicit answers.

Improving final thoughts

Option 1

To review "Writing a final thought" from Unit 1 Part 2, elicit:

1. *What should the last part of a concluding paragraph be?* (Answer: **A final thought**)

2. *What are the different types of final thoughts that can be used?* (Answer: **Opinion, solution, recommendation, prediction**)

3. *What should a final thought not do?* (Answer: **Introduce a new idea**)

Option 2

1. Have students read the explanation and the example on page 110. Do not have students read the explanation on page 111 yet.

2. Have students discuss with a partner:
   • *What is wrong with the final thought?*

3. Then have students compare their answers with those given in the explanation on page 111.

4. Note that the style of the final thought required for an essay in English may be very different from the students' own language. Explain that the final thought needs to be precise, objective (not emotional or an emotional appeal), and related to the thesis.

5. Emphasize:
   • *An effective final thought is essential because it is the writer's last chance to make an impact on the reader.*

Exercise 2

Option 1

1. Divide the class into pairs.

2. Have students work collaboratively to complete the exercise.

3. Elicit answers.

Option 2

1. Follow Option 1 above.

2. Then have pairs identify the weaknesses of the ineffective final thoughts.

3. Elicit answers.

Section 2 — Revising a compare and contrast essay

Option 1

1. Have students read the checklist.

2. Encourage students to clarify the meaning of any items with a partner or the teacher. This is a good opportunity to review the material that has been covered.

Option 2

1. Have students read the checklist.

2. As students are reading, write the following on the board:

   First draft checklist:
   • *Whole essay*
   • *Introductory paragraph*
   • *Body paragraphs*
   • *Concluding paragraph*
   • *Language/coherence*

3. Then have students, in pairs or small groups and with books closed, try to recall the questions in each checklist category.

4. Elicit answers to the following:
   - *What are questions you can ask about the whole essay?*
   - *What are questions you can ask about the introductory paragraph?*
   - *What are questions you can ask about the body paragraphs?*
   - *What are questions you can ask about the concluding paragraph?*
   - *What are questions you can ask about language and coherence?*
   (Answers: See textbook page 113, checklist)

Exercise 3

Option 1

1. Divide the class into pairs or small groups.

2. Have students work collaboratively to edit the essay category by category on the checklist. Remind students that editing is about identifying the positives (what is successful) as much as the negatives.

3. After each category/paragraph, elicit edits/key points.

Option 2

1. Follow Option 1 above.

2. Have the pairs/groups discuss:
   - *Do you agree with the writer's ideas?*

3. Elicit answers.

Exercise 4

Option 1

1. Divide the class into small groups.

2. Have them work collaboratively to answer the questions for Essay A.

3. Elicit answers.

4. Then have students answer the questions for Essay B individually.

5. Have students compare their answers with their group members.

6. Elicit answers.

Option 2

1. Divide the class into pairs (Pair A and Pair B).

2. Have:
   - Pair A work together to answer the questions about Essay A.
   - Pair B work together to answer the questions about Essay B.

3. Then have each Pair A sit with a Pair B and explain their answers to each other.

4. Elicit answers.

Answer Key

UNIT 1 PART 1

Exercise 1

<u>p. 5</u>

1. **Introduction** = the first paragraph
   Body = the second, third, and fourth paragraphs
   Conclusion = the fifth paragraph

2. **Hook** = *"I'd put my money on the sun and solar energy. What a source of power! I hope we don't have to wait until oil and coal run out before we tackle that."*

   Building sentences = *With this statement, Thomas Edison, the inventor of the light bulb, recognized the capacity of the sun as a virtually limitless source of energy in 1931. However, although a time when oil and coal have been completely used up could be getting closer, the full potential of solar power is yet to be harnessed by mankind. Televisions, refrigerators, air conditioners, and all the other appliances common in the developed world require vast amounts of electricity, meaning that the world's most powerful countries still very much depend on fossil fuels. In Sub-Saharan Africa, Southeast Asia, and parts of South America, however, solar power is already changing the lives of people who have until now lived without a steady electricity supply. As low-cost solar panels become available, they are being used most effectively in some of the world's poorest countries, which also happen to be some of the sunniest.*

   Thesis statement = *Solar power is improving people's lives in developing countries by providing efficient light safely, linking them to the global mobile community and increasing their independence.*

3. <u>Body paragraph 1</u>
   Topic sentence = *Low-cost, solar-powered lamps provide a dependable and safe source of light to people in rural communities who often have no connection to a national electricity grid.*

   Supporting sentences = *People either had to do without electricity, or were limited to using unreliable, low-intensity light from candles or kerosene lamps at night. Now, a new solar-powered lamp, when charged for eight hours in the bright sun, can provide up to a hundred hours of continuous, stable light ("Solar"). As a result, families are now able to extend and enrich their days by pursuing hobbies or crafts, and socializing longer into the evening with a brighter, constant light. Furthermore, solar power is clean and safe. An Energy Resource Group article reports, "Health problems caused by toxic fumes from kerosene lamps are responsible for an estimated two million deaths annually" (Silver). In addition, both candles and kerosene are a fire hazard, especially in homes that tend to be predominantly made of wood. Solar-powered lighting removes these dangers from people's homes because they emit no fumes and have no open flame, so people*

   benefit from cleaner air and a reduced worry of fire.

   Concluding sentence = *Solar power, therefore, has not only changed people's lives, it has also made their lives safer.*

   <u>Body paragraph 2</u>
   Topic sentence = *As well as providing reliable and safe light, the power of these solar panels is also being used to help people in developing countries connect to global communication networks.*

   Supporting sentences = *The same solar panel that provides light at night can be used to charge and recharge a cellular phone, which brings a number of significant benefits. For example, New York Times writer Sharon LaFraniere found that in rural, often remote parts of Sub-Saharan Africa, cell phones allow people to communicate easily and immediately with neighboring villages, as well as provide access to banking networks and global information sources (C3). The same article also reported that in a study of rural communities in developing countries, shop owners, traders, farmers, and fishermen all claimed that access to a cell phone had a positive impact on their profits (LaFraniere C3). As a result, their communities benefited economically.*

   Concluding sentence = *By providing a link to the world beyond the old limits of their immediate community, solar power is giving people in developing nations the means to improve their livelihoods.*

   <u>Body paragraph 3</u>
   Topic sentence = *Last, as a consequence of the technological benefits brought by solar power, people in developing countries are able to live their lives with greater autonomy.*

   Supporting sentences = *Solar power allows a poor family to make considerable financial savings. A BBC news story explains that a solar-powered lamp is relatively expensive for most families in developing countries, but because it costs nothing to operate after the purchase, it is much cheaper than alternatives, like kerosene ("Solar"). With their savings, more families can invest money into developing or expanding their farms or small businesses, which leads to greater financial stability and independence. Furthermore, solar power provides an environment in which people can educate themselves. In the journal Africa Renewal – United Nations Department of Public Information, it was concluded that literacy rates and the number of people studying for trade certificates are increasing faster in towns and villages where solar-powered lamps are accessible (Madamombe 10).*

   Concluding sentence = *Therefore, by allowing both children and adults to study at home in the evenings, solar power provides an opportunity for many people in the poorest parts of the world to escape a life of dependency through better education.*

4. **Restated thesis** = *In summary, solar power is making a significant difference in the lives of people in the developing world.*

Summary of main ideas = *By providing safe, clean, and efficient light, it is removing dangers from people's homes while brightening their evenings. In addition, the ability to charge a cell phone allows people to communicate with the world and grow their businesses. The increased time and money available give people the means to take control of their lives and build for the future.*

Final thought = *The evidence certainly shows that in parts of the world where there is abundant sunlight, harnessing solar energy can be a key to improving the lives of many people.*

Exercise 2

p. 8

1. ✓

   Topic: *South Korean dramas*
   Writer's position: (South Korean dramas) *are popular*
   Main ideas: *the traditional values in these shows, the focus on romantic love, the kindness of the male characters*

2. ✗

   Topic: *smartphones*
   Writer's position: unclear
   Main ideas: *allow us to connect to the internet, provide a range of useful and entertaining applications, combine the functions of several electronic devices*

3. ✗

   Topic: *The internet*
   Writer's position: unclear
   Main ideas: *has caused interest in daily newspapers to fall; may cause some newspapers to close*

4. ✗

   Topic: *Popular music*
   Writer's position: (Popular music) *changed dramatically in the 1990s*
   Main ideas: unclear ("for a number of reasons" is not specific enough)

5. ✗

   Topic: *contemporary American comics*
   Writer's position: (contemporary American comics) are not formulaic because they *cover a wide range of interests and themes*
   Main ideas: *history; social problems; human relationships*

Exercise 3

p. 9

1. 3

2. 5

3. 2

4. 1

5. 4

Exercise 4

p. 9

c, e

(Explanation)

c and **e** are appropriate choices because the following sentence states, "*One growing trend worldwide against **this way of life** is the 'slow life' movement, . . .*" The hook needs to be a referent for the expression *"this way of life,"* and it needs to express the idea that is opposite to slow life. Both **c** and **e** express the idea of people's lives being busy; therefore, either of them makes an appropriate hook. **a**, **b**, and **d** are not appropriate choices because they do not clearly include the idea of people's lives being busy; they do not make a good contrast to the idea of "slow life."

Exercise 5

p. 11

1. 1st "Although this . . ."
   2nd "Yoga classes . . ."
   3rd "They are drawn . . ."

2. 1st "Described as . . ."
   2nd "The ongoing . . ."
   3rd "This success . . ."

Exercise 6

p. 12

Answers will vary.

(Example answers)

1. (Chronological pattern)
   • First use of nuclear weapons
   • Other countries gain nuclear technology
   • Cold war
   • Nuclear non-proliferation treaty
   • Developing countries gaining the technology

The following is an example of how the above points could be expressed in the actual building sentences: She was articulating what she considers to be a practical reaction to the realities of the existence of such weapons. Since the first use of nuclear weapons in 1945, the world has lived in fear of the awesome destructive power of these weapons. Following this, other nations such as France, China, and the U.K., also developed such technology. Indeed, the cold war between the United States and the Soviet Union was so terrifying precisely because both nations possessed such enormous nuclear arsenals. Despite attempts at non-proliferation treaties, in more recent years developing countries have also begun to, or attempted to, acquire nuclear weapons.

2. (General to specific pattern)
    Year overseas is a serious decision
    Advantages in a globalized world
    Some problems involved in study abroad
    Maybe a waste of time
    It is a popular choice today

The following is an example of how the preceding points could be expressed in the actual building sentences:

Devoting a whole year of university time to life in another country is a significant decision to make. As the world increasingly globalizes, the advantages of gaining this kind of experience are obvious. However, the practicalities involved present problems of cost, homesickness, and safety, in addition to the fact that students might more usefully spend this time in their own country concentrating on their chosen degree course. Nevertheless, it appears that this is not enough to put young people off the idea.

UNIT 1 PART 2

Exercise 1

p. 14

1. ✓

    Topic: *sources of revenue for Thailand*
    Controlling idea: *One major source of revenue for Thailand is food*

2. ✗

    Topic: *unclear* (The second reason for "what" is unclear)
    Controlling idea: *young people can use their laptops for tablets while drinking coffee*

3. ✗

    Topic: *unclear* (Ghost stories need more information, e.g., the roles of ghost stories, the purposes for telling ghost stories, etc.)
    Controlling idea: *reveal the traditional differences in social status between men and women*

4. ✗

    Topic: *the reason why* Bolivar *did something*
    Controlling idea: *unclear* (it is unclear what *this* refers to)

5. ✓

    Topic: *problems with wind power turbines*
    Controlling idea: (*Another problem with wind power turbines is that*) *they often kill birds and bats*

Exercise 2

p. 15

a. evidence

b. Explanation

    Smoking causes a number of problems in restaurants. Firstly, smoking can damage the health of people who work in restaurants. According to government research, working for four hours in a restaurant that permits smoking is the same as smoking six cigarettes. **More evidence is a recent report in the** Journal of Medical Science**, which found that workers in smoking environments were more likely to develop cancer**. *This shows that people who work in such restaurants for many years are exposed to risks that they cannot control. In addition, smoke can reduce customers' enjoyment of visiting a restaurant. For example, if smoke gets into people's mouths, they are less sensitive to taste, and particles of smoke may overpower delicate foods. For many people, the chance to eat delicious food is a reason for going to a restaurant, but cigarette smoke often spoils that chance.* **As well, cigarette smoke causes many people to feel nauseous**. *Therefore, a smoking ban in all restaurants would allow employees and customers to feel comfortable because their health and ability to enjoy the experience would be better protected.*

Exercise 3

p. 17

1. T-1-2-3-1-2-3-C

2. T-1-2-1-3-2-1-2-C

Exercise 4

p. 18

(Example answers)

1. In conclusion, the youth culture of the United States has had an important effect on young people's lifestyles worldwide.

2. To summarize, the popularity of yoga for young women has increased in recent times.

3. In short, smartphones have shown they are more than just a method of communicating and can now be used for other practical everyday situations.

Exercise 5

p. 19

1. solution/recommendation

2. prediction/speculation

3. opinion/judgment

(Explanation)

1. *need to* suggests recommendation

2. *It is likely that* and *will remain stable* express the writer's prediction

3. *It seems* implies the writer's opinion that one idea can be applied to another situation

Exercise 6

p. 20

1. c

2. c

(Explanation)

1. **c** is the most appropriate ending because it expresses the writer's recommendation after considering the benefits of young children taking music lessons, which are the main points of this essay. **a** is not an appropriate ending because the writer is making a negative prediction about the number of children who will take music lessons in the future, which is contrary to the previous information in the paragraph that concentrates on benefits. **b** is not an appropriate ending because it includes an idea that was never presented in the body of the essay. Neither the restated thesis nor summary of the main points mentions the government's responsibility to spend more money on music lessons in schools.

2. **c** is the most appropriate ending because it expresses the writer's prediction/speculation based on the ideas presented in the essay. **a** is not an effective ending because the writer is presenting an inappropriate opinion/judgment (*"People should realize that real beauty does not lie in a person's appearance but in their mind."*), whereas the restated thesis is simply stating the fact that cosmetic surgery is becoming more acceptable to people for a variety of reasons. **b** is not an appropriate ending because it includes an idea that was never presented in the body of the essay (*"there are many TV programs and websites which introduce people who have had cosmetic surgery and who explain how much their surgery cost"*). The remaining information is also ineffective because it is based on this new idea.

Exercise 7

p. 22

OUTLINE

Topic: *Solar power*

Thesis statement:
Solar power is improving people's lives in developing countries by providing efficient light safely, linking them to the global mobile community and increasing their independence.

Body Paragraph 1

Topic sentence:
Low-cost, solar-powered lamps provide a dependable and safe source of light to people in rural communities who often have no connection to a national electricity grid.

Supporting points:
1. *Solar power extends/enriches people's days*
2. *Solar power is clean and safe*

Body Paragraph 2

Topic sentence:
As well as providing reliable and safe light, the power of these solar panels is also being used to help people in developing countries connect to global communication networks.

Supporting points:
1. *People can communicate with neighboring villages with cell phones charged with solar panels*
2. *Shop owners, traders, farmers, fishermen have positive impacts on their business with cell phones*

Body Paragraph 3

Topic sentence:
Last, as a consequence of the technological benefits brought by solar power, people in developing countries are able to live their lives with greater autonomy.

Supporting points:
1. *Solar-powered lamps are affordable*
2. *Solar power provides an environment in which people can educate themselves*

UNIT 1 PART 3

Exercise 1

p. 26

The whole essay

1. Yes.

2. Mostly yes, but the writer uses some subjective language that makes the tone of writing less objective (see **Comments** below).

3. Mostly yes, but it contains some irrelevant information (see **Comments** below).

Introductory paragraph

4. Yes, but it is not interesting enough to make the reader want to continue reading, and it is also overgeneralized.

5. Yes.

6. It includes the topic ("the internet") and the writer's position ("the internet has a significant impact on people's lives"), but it does not contain the main ideas of each body paragraph, and the unnecessary addition of the phrase *of the internet* in it also results in confusing meaning.

Body paragraphs

7. No (see **Comments** below).

8. Mostly yes, but there is one irrelevant idea at the end of body paragraph 2 (see **Comments** below).

9. Yes in body paragraph 1, but not so effectively in body paragraphs 2 and 3.

Concluding paragraph

10. No.

11. Yes, but it could be more elaborate (see **Comments** below).

12. No.

13. No (see **Comments** below).

Comments:
- The writer uses the subjective phrase *I think* at the end of body paragraph 1. This should be eliminated to create a more objective tone in writing.
- There is irrelevant information at the end of body paragraph 2. *"It is also good for the environment as it reduces how much people have to travel to do their shopping. Clearly if fewer people need to go into a city to do their shopping, then less pollution will be produced"* is irrelevant because this idea is not directly related to the paragraph's controlling idea, which is the change that occurred in business because of the internet.
- The topic sentences in the body paragraphs do not contain the necessary elements effectively (see Unit 1 Part 2, page 13). The topic sentence in body paragraph 1 does not state the topic clearly (it is unclear what *It* indicates). The topic sentence in body paragraph 2 needs to state the controlling idea more specifically, e.g., **how** the internet has changed business. The topic sentence in body paragraph 3 does not state the topic clearly (Why is it now possible to communicate with people more easily?).
- The summary of the main points can be separated into three sentences, which summarize the three body paragraphs with a little more details respectively (see how the summary of the main points is presented in the model essay in Unit 1 Part 1, page 6).
- The concluding paragraph is not effective because it has a new idea. *"However, it is important to note that there are many other ways in which the internet has affected people's lives, such as giving them the ability to download music and movies, play online games, and find new friends."* This idea was never discussed in the body of the essay; thus, it should never appear in the conclusion. The writer should avoid ending the essay with a new idea because it makes the reader think that the essay is not really completed.

(Example of a corrected draft **boldfacing** indicates added or changed parts, and ~~crossed out~~ items are to be removed)

The Impact of the Internet on People's Lives
Few people today can imagine life without the internet. Recently it has become common for people, not only in developed, but also developing countries to have it. It is no longer seen as something that is only used by people who are interested in computers, but it has become a part of modern life. The internet is having a significant impact ~~of the internet~~ on people's lives **by making information more easily available, improving shopping opportunities, and enhancing communication among family and friends**.

Firstly, **the internet** has allowed people to access information very easily. In the past, people could only learn about current events from newspapers that were sold where they lived, or by watching the news that was shown on their televisions. The internet has changed this. Now people are able to be much more informed about world events. As well, people are able to learn about topics that they are interested in much more easily. For example free online encyclopedias make it possible to get information on almost any subject. In addition students can easily find relevant resources, such as academic articles, for their studies. Consequently, they are able to write better essays. Therefore, ~~I think that~~ it is clear that the internet makes people more informed about the world around them.

Secondly, the internet has improved **shopping by increasing product variety and available product information for consumers**. For example online retailers, such as Amazon, stock a wide range of goods. Rather than customers having to visit shops in order to buy the products that they want, it is now possible for them to view and buy a large range of goods from the comfort of their homes. This is a great thing as it means that people in rural areas, who in the past did not have access to a wide variety of products, can now enjoy shopping just like people who live in big cities. ~~It is also good for the environment as it reduces how much people have to travel to do their shopping. Clearly if fewer people need to go into a city to do their shopping, then less pollution will be produced.~~ **Another advantage of online shopping is that online reviews can help buyers make educated purchasing choices. Most reputable internet-based sellers invite customers to review products purchased from them, and such evaluations can be extremely useful for potential shoppers to select items and verify claims made by manufacturers. This increased range of easily available products whose quality can be ascertained was created by the internet.**

Finally, it is now possible to communicate with people more easily **because the internet allows people to exchange various types of information inexpensively and instantly**. In the past, living far apart from friends and family made it difficult and expensive to keep in contact, but the internet provides people with a number of cheap and easy ways to keep in touch. For example, people can use email to send letters and photos to people who are on the other side of the world. It is also possible for them use video conferencing applications to see and talk to people irrespective of the distance between them. As a result, people no longer feel that moving to a different city, country, or even continent will lead to less communication with their friends and families. **Thus, because of the internet, people's financial situation and the distance between them have become less relevant to successful communication.**

In conclusion, the internet **has improved the way people live in various ways. It has increased the availability and range of various types of information. It has allowed shoppers to buy** almost anything without needing to leave home. The internet has also improved communication opportunities between friends and loved ones. ~~However it is important to note that there are many other ways in which the internet has affected people's lives, such as giving them the ability to download music and movies, play online games, and find new friends.~~ With all these positive contributions to one's quality of life, the spread of the internet all over the globe is a phenomenon that will be welcomed by most people.

Exercise 2

p. 29

(Corrected parts are underlined.)
Modern Youth Trends
In the last three decades, people's lifestyles have changed dramatically. Today, it seems that more and more people are pursuing individual <u>happiness rather</u> than collective satisfaction, and this trend is more apparent among young people. Now, many people who have graduated from school choose part-time employment and do not attend university. Researchers and scientists do not know why. However, one theory states that young people today feel <u>unmotivated because</u> parents work longer away from home and they could not give the guidance children need.

Exercise 3

p. 30

(Corrected parts are ~~crossed out~~ or underlined.)
Many people like <u>YouTube because</u> it has many funny videos of people just like themselves. ~~YouTube has become very popular~~ People laugh the most when they see <u>something about a situation that is strange, or someone who is very familiar to them.</u> <u>For example,</u> when people see a cat swinging from curtains and a woman in a beautiful dress falling into a wedding cake, <u>they laugh because</u> they understand the situation. ~~And~~ They <u>also</u> laugh since ~~they~~ these events are real ~~but~~ <u>and</u> not a script from a comedian, which is also funny ~~but~~ for another reason ~~but~~ not really related to everyday life.

UNIT 2 PART 1

Exercise 1

p. 33

Authority: written by employees of Waseda University International, all teachers of academic writing, so should have some knowledge of the field!

Purpose: to inform the reader, specifically to instruct students in how to write effective academic essays

Intended audience: for university students learning to write academic English

Relevance: published in 2012, so up to date

Exercise 2

p. 36

One of the clearest examples of <u>animal culture</u> can be found in the behavior of a group of <u>bottlenose dolphins</u> in <u>Shark Bay, Australia</u>. The <u>dolphins</u> pick up <u>sea sponges</u> from the bottom of the <u>sea</u> and wear them on their <u>noses</u> for protection when looking for <u>food</u>. Of a total <u>130 dolphins</u> living in the area, only one extended <u>family group</u> of around <u>20</u> displays this behavior (MacLure 78). This suggests that the use of the <u>sponges</u> as a tool is being learned and passed on within the <u>group</u>.

Exercise 3

p. 37

a is the best. It is the closest in length to the original, both vocabulary and structure are sufficiently changed, none of the shared language is missing, and there are no missing points or added ideas (with the possible exception of *accentuated*, which was not in the original).

b attempts structure and vocabulary changes in various places, but it is still too similar to the original at several places. Although it is only borderline lexical plagiarism because shared language is involved, parts such as "influenced by jazz and rhythm and blues," "radio stations from," and "cities such as New Orleans" could easily be changed. Also, the idea of "traditional" referring to Caribbean music was not in the original.

c has missing information, namely that the new ska was "influenced by jazz and rhythm and blues." Also, saying that local musicians "copied" music is an oversimplification.

Exercise 4

p. 37

(Example answers)

1. (59-word original; 55-word paraphrase)
   Caribbean communities are integral parts of British society today. Caribbean immigrants started arriving in great numbers and contributing to the U.K. workforce in the wake of the Second World War. Although they came with the hope of improving their quality of life, initially many faced shortages of work and accommodation in addition to encountering racism.

2. (53-word original; 60-word paraphrase)
   The annual number of visitors to the two-day-long Notting Hill Carnival has exceeded two million, making it the second greatest street festival in the world. Celebrated in the Notting Hill region of London every August, it is dedicated to Caribbean arts and culture brought by Caribbean immigrants, many of whom first took up residence in this part of the city.

3. (49-word original; 52-word paraphrase)
   A more aggressive and harder style of ska music was born in the U.K. at the end of the 1970s fusing old ska with punk or rock. Creators of this new version formed groups with multiethnic compositions which fostered harmony among races along with their songs which brought racial problems to light.

Exercise 5

p. 38

b is the best. It is a short and accurate summary of the reasons for and the consequences of the "demise of aboriginal cultures."

a is perhaps a little too long, and it introduces the new idea that "the world risks losing forever its valuable diversity."

c is an incomplete summary as it focuses only on one point: the value of aboriginal cultures. It ignores the fact that these cultures are under threat.

Exercise 6

p. 39

(Example answers)
1. (67-word original; 24-word paraphrase)
   Indigenous people are the first inhabitants populating a certain area possessing distinct language, culture, and traditions setting them apart from the later dominant group.

2. (90-word original; 27-word paraphrase)
   Thousands of indigenous groups exist today spread over many countries. Deprived of their land and resources, these surviving groups often cannot continue their traditional ways of living.

3. (86-word original; 33-word paraphrase)
   Plagued by poverty and various other problems, many Native Americans in the U.S. abandoned their traditional lifestyles. They exemplify the common phenomenon of indigenous peoples being the poorest ethnic groups in a country.

UNIT 2 PART 2

Exercise 1

p. 43

1. No.
2. Yes. Specific figures coming from research always need to be cited.
3. No, because the observations are not specific.
4. No. This is common geographical knowledge.
5. No. This is common historical/scientific knowledge.
6. Yes because specific data is included.

Exercise 2

p. 46

1. Six
2. The six instances are as follows:
   1) Now, a new solar-powered lamp, when charged for eight hours in the bright sun, can provide up to a hundred hours of continuous, stable light.
   2) "Health problems caused by toxic fumes from kerosene lamps are responsible for an estimated two million deaths annually."
   3) . . . in rural, often remote parts of Sub-Saharan Africa, cell phones allow people to communicate easily and immediately with neighboring villages, as well as provide access to banking networks and global information sources.
   4) . . . in a study of rural communities in developing countries, shop owners, traders, farmers, and fishermen all claimed that access to a cell phone had a positive impact on their profits.
   5) . . . a solar-powered lamp is relatively expensive for most families in developing countries, but because it costs nothing to operate after the purchase, it is much cheaper than alternatives, like kerosene.
   6) . . . literacy rates and the number of people studying for trade certificates are increasing faster in towns and villages where solar-powered lamps are accessible.
3. The five introductory phrases are as follows (the first citation did not have one):
   1) An Energy Resource Group article reports, . . . (Silver).
   2) . . . *New York Times* writer Sharon LaFraniere found that . . . (C3).
   3) The same article also reported that . . . (LaFraniere C3).
   4) A BBC news story explains that . . . ("Solar").
   5) In the journal *Africa Renewal – United Nations Department of Public Information*, it was concluded that . . . (Madamombe 10).
4. In alphabetical order.
5. Yes.
6. "Solar Loans Light Up Rural India" from BBC News is cited as "Solar" because when the author is unknown, the first word(s) of the title should be used between quotation marks.
7. In order to give extra authority to the source. This is useful when the author is not so well known or when he or she is not an established expert on the topic.
8. Always the first piece of information presented in its Works Cited entry along with the page number when available. Examples in order of appearance:
   • ("Solar")
   • (Silver)

- Sharon LaFraniere . . . (C3)
- (LaFraniere C3)
- ("Solar")
- (Madamombe 10)

9.
- The first citation ("Solar") uses Pattern 2. In this case, the information is emphasized over its source.
- The second citation (Silver) uses Pattern 1 because the source is clearly an authority, so this pattern is more efficient.
- The third citation (LaFraniere) uses Pattern 1 to emphasize that this author is a reliable source of information.
- The fourth citation (LaFraniere) uses Pattern 1 to emphasize that this author is a reliable source of information.
- The fifth citation ("Solar") uses Pattern 1 to give more authority to the source that was cited in Pattern 2 at the beginning of the essay.
- The sixth citation (Madamombe) uses Pattern 1 because the source is clearly an authority, so this pattern is more efficient.

Exercise 3

p. 50

(Example answer)

Although more books are being bought than ever before in history, these books are not being read. One reason is that many people buy books in order to find specific pieces of information that they need for their jobs and hobbies.This has led to a large number of specialized books being published. **For instance, in 2004, 15% of books that were published in the U.K. were scientific or technical ("No End" 9)**. One consequence of this is that many books are used only as a reference and they are not read from cover to cover. Also, people buy books that they think they should read, but often do not find enough time to finish them. **As Joseph Hunter notes, a large number of the self-help books that are bought are never read (67–68)**. Although people seem to have the intention of reading books, they clearly lack the motivation to actually sit down and spend time reading them. Furthermore, people collect books as status symbols to show their knowledge. **"Reading books has given way to the status of possessing books," observes literary critic Malcolm Riggs (qtd. in Davinder)**. This shows that people are buying books, not for the pleasure of reading them, but rather because they feel that simply owning them has a positive effect. Clearly people are still motivated to buy books, but many do not have the desire to actually read them; this may partly be due to the other forms of entertainment that are available to them.

Exercise 4

p. 53

Works Cited

Nigeria. Office of Public Communication. *Quality Education Central to Our Agenda for National Transformation*. 18 May 2011. Web. 19 June 2011. <http://www.nigeriafirst.org/article_11089.shtml>.

Packer, George. "Knowing the Enemy." *The New Yorker* 18 Dec. 2006: 60–69. Print.

Tatum, Beverly Daniel. *Why Are All the Black Kids Sitting Together in the Cafeteria?* New York: Basic Books. 1997. Print.

"World's Education Leaders: Support Teachers." *AskAsia.org*. 2011. Asia Society. Web. 12 Apr. 2011. < http://asiasociety.org/education-learning/ learning-world/worlds-education-leaderssupport-teachers>.

UNIT 3 PART 1

Exercise 1

p. 56

1. Wikipedia.
2. Wikipedia provides a useful starting point for research.

Exercise 2

p. 61

Answers will vary.

(Example answers)

1. Students with no interest in study abroad will perform badly and so waste a year of their university lives.

2. This puts too much focus on students performing well to get a future career, but students need to value their studies more as a chance to develop intellectually.

3. A high athletic ability is unrelated to intellectual ability, so these students may have great difficulties studying in higher education.

Exercise 3

p. 63

1. The second rebuttal is more effective. It is focused on the idea of "freedom to discuss personal interests" and argues against its value, giving a reason in support ("limiting a student's chances to develop").

   The first rebuttal does not directly address the counter-argument. Instead of "personal interests," it discusses "talking with more people." Moreover, the support does not seem logical (why would "talking with more people" allow a student to "develop quicker"?).

2. The first rebuttal is more effective. It concedes that teachers "may have" a good understanding of their students' weakness, but asserts that this is also true in group classes. Continuing this point, it adds a disadvantage of private classes, showing how they may be "demotivating."

The second rebuttal does not address the central idea of the counter-argument (that teachers in private classes have "a better understanding of their students' strengths and weaknesses"). Instead, it focuses on (nonspecific) "pressure" in private classes and also the "strong listening skills" of group class students (which are both unsupported).

Exercise 4

p. 63

Answers will vary.

(Example answers)

1. Even students who have "no interest" at first might have a rewarding experience, and all students are sure to learn a lot from living in a foreign country.

2. "Developing intellectually" is too abstract an idea and so unlikely to motivate many students. It would be more effective to focus on something more practical, such as future career prospects.

3. Perhaps some of these students will be challenged intellectually, but being a successful athlete requires rigorous discipline and perseverance, and having these traits can help them catch up with smarter students.

Exercise 5

p. 64

1. Framework A.

2. **Counter-argument 1:** *Those who are in favor of private lessons may argue that students can learn better in this style because they can "customize" their lessons.*
   Rebuttal: *However, it has been observed that at the beginner level, what students in group lessons learn is not different from that learned by students in private lessons.*
   Counter-argument 2: *Another objection to group lessons may be that group learners have less opportunity to interact with teachers.*
   Rebuttal: *According to a study which examined private language lessons, 70% of the conversation is dominated by the instructors.*

3.

OUTLINE

Thesis statement:
However, in reality, group lessons are more effective for language learning because they allow students to learn from each other and provide a supportive atmosphere, both of which are vital in successful language acquisition.

Body Paragraph 1
Topic sentence:
First, it can be clearly seen that peer-learning, where students learn directly from each other, is essential in foreign language learning.

Supporting points:
From peer interaction, students learn various skills:
- negotiate meaning
- start and control discussions
- use a variety of expressions

Body Paragraph 2
Topic sentence:
Furthermore, it is apparent that a positive group atmosphere helps students to learn a foreign language.

Supporting points:
Group environment is:
- *not intimidating, not exhausting*
- *Encouragement from peers is a "fabulous motivator"*

Body Paragraph 3
Counter-arguments:
Counter-argument 1: *Those who are in favor of private lessons may argue that students can learn better in this style because they can "customize" their lessons.*
Counter-argument 2: *Another objection to group lessons may be that group learners have less opportunity to interact with teachers.*

Rebuttals:
Rebuttal 1: *However, it has been observed that at the beginner level, what students in group lessons learn is not different from that learned by students in private lessons.*

Rebuttal 2: *According to a study which examined private language lessons, 70% of the conversation is dominated by the instructors.*

Exercise 6

p. 68

OUTLINE

Thesis statement:
However, in reality, group lessons are more effective for language learning because they allow students to learn from each other and provide a supportive atmosphere, both of which are vital in successful language acquisition.

Body Paragraph 1
Argument 1 (topic sentence):
There is evidence that peer-learning, learning from other students, is essential in foreign language acquisition.

Counter-argument 1:
A student can learn the skills needed to communicate in a target language more effectively from a teacher in private lessons.

Rebuttals to counter-argument:
From peer interaction, students learn various skills:
- negotiating meaning
- starting or controlling discussions
- using a variety of expressions

<u>Body Paragraph 2</u>

Argument 2 (topic sentence):
Another advantage of group lessons is that it can create a less stressful atmosphere, which is also desirable in foreign language learning.

Counter-argument 2:
. . . a teacher's being able to provide constant attention and support to a student is a significant advantage in private lessons.

Rebuttals to counter-argument:
Group environment is:
- *less daunting or tiring*
- *no "non-stop spotlight of the instructor's attention"*
- *desirable option for people who do not learn well in stressful situations*

UNIT 3 PART 2

Exercise 1

p. 72

1. Direct thesis
2. Some, however, claim such thinking is naive and fundamentally flawed due to the belief that a reliance on amateur editors will lead to inaccurate and unreliable entires.

Exercise 2

p. 73

(Example answer; **boldfacing** indicates changed parts)
As the internet gained popularity, many hoped it would develop as a decentralizing and democratizing force where people could share information and learn from each other. Wikipedia, a free online encyclopedia and the world's largest reference resource, embodies such ideals in allowing multiple users to write and revise content. This collaborative practice differs from the process of compiling conventional encyclopedias, which relies on scholars and experts to contribute information. Wikipedia's underlying belief is that by having more participants contributing and editing information, **entries demonstrate a comprehensive overview of complex topics, a neutral editorial stance, and a dedicated commitment to quality**. Some, however, claim such thinking is naïve and fundamentally flawed due to the belief that a reliance on amateur editors will lead to inaccurate and unreliable entries. Yet, Wikipedia **remains a useful starting point for research through its greater range, depth, and accuracy of each entry.**

Exercise 3

p. 75

Note: Alternate words and phrases are purposely used in the model essay to highlight the many ways to introduce arguments.

The Democratizing of Knowledge: in Defense of Wikipedia

As the internet gained popularity, many hoped it would develop as a decentralizing and democratizing force where people could share information and learn from each other. Wikipedia, a free online encyclopedia and the world's largest reference resource, embodies such ideals in allowing multiple users to write and revise content. This collaborative practice differs from the process of compiling conventional encyclopedias, which relies on scholars and experts to contribute information. Wikipedia's underlying belief is that by having more participants contributing and editing information, each entry will have greater range, depth, and accuracy. <u>Some</u>, however, <u>claim</u> such thinking is naïve and fundamentally flawed due to the belief that a reliance on amateur editors will lead to inaccurate and unreliable entries. Yet, Wikipedia does provide a useful starting point for research, offering a comprehensive overview of complex topics, a neutral editorial stance, and a dedicated commitment to quality.

Launched in 2001, Wikipedia has become a valuable resource of information in a relatively short amount of time. <u>One reason</u> for this quick growth and for its reliability is the collective participation of a vast range of contributors from around the world. The number of people who contribute or edit information on Wikipedia is in the hundreds of thousands (Soneff). Furthermore, these contributions have to be facts that are verifiable, and entries must be unbiased and based on secondary research. Researchers at Dartmouth College concluded that these large numbers and the rules for contribution indicate that Wikipedia users are accessing information which is constantly being updated and checked for errors, therefore ensuring the information is accurate, which is a feature not available with traditional encyclopedias. <u>Wikipedia's value is also evident</u> in the breadth of information available. Olivia Solon, news editor at Wired.co.uk states that Wikipedia carries over 3.5 million entries across a diverse variety of topics ranging from the technical to the trivial. Furthermore, Wikipedia features hyperlinks within entries to related topics/terms, providing users with direct access to additional sources which may lead to a deeper understanding of a topic. Moreover, Wikipedia is not exclusive to those who can read English: not only is it one of the most frequented websites in the world, but it is also a multilingual resource with 270 non-English Wikipedia sites ("User-generated"). <u>The result is</u> a website which is a useful "one-stop" resource for research across disciplines and languages. The success of Wikipedia, therefore, has democratized knowledge through its vast amount of accurate and up-to-date information, and through its belief that any responsible user or contributor can access and add knowledge for the benefit of all people.

Together with its vast scope, the principle **that all Wikipedia entries should be comprehensive and balanced makes it** an especially valuable research tool. Academic research involves grappling with complex issues, concepts, or events, which is precisely what Wikipedia does. For example, the term *globalization* is especially controversial. For many, globalization means exploitation and widespread injustice (Scheve and Slaughter 4); for others, globalization is a beneficial force (Wolf 36). This disparity means it is especially important for researchers to comprehensively understand why the term is so controversial. Wikipedia, with its large number of contributors representing a range of possible points of view, provides detailed descriptions, the variety of perspectives on the issue, and the reasons for the controversy. Wikipedia's policy also ensures that neutrality is maintained, which is crucial for academic research on issues which are fiercely contested. Globalization issues involve pro-globalization and anti-globalization arguments, but both sides are described comprehensively in the Wikipedia entry on the topic. Indeed, this is only possible because **Wikipedia is a free, Web-based resource that presents** the breadth and depth of meanings associated with complex, contentious terms in a balanced way. **This accessibility to unbiased information helps** ensure that research results are accurate because the user is able to analyze and carefully consider all sides of an issue.

Despite such benefits, **Wikipedia continues to attract critics, who claim** there are significant weaknesses with its philosophy of complete openness. **One** perceived **weakness is** with the contributors, many of whom are not scholars or experts on the topics to which they add or alter information. **The worry is** that Wikipedia, by having entries which anyone can edit, is not a dependable resource because it is filled with incorrect, biased information ("Wikipedia"). Nevertheless, Wikipedia does employ a dedicated team of volunteer administrators whose job it is to quickly remedy inaccurate information. Furthermore, controversial entries can be tagged to indicate when information is under dispute and to encourage users to investigate the dispute and provide more input. Professor of communications Jonathan Thornton maintains that "the service revolves around a set of procedures that are carefully designed to ensure accurate articles through sufficient self-policing and self-amending." A study by the journal *Nature* indeed showed that Wikipedia is nearly as accurate as *Britannica* (Giles 900). A further concern is over vandalism of entries with false, malicious information, often aiming to hurt the reputation of certain people or organizations. However, this matter is being addressed through various measures. For example, software is being developed to swiftly detect words not consistent with the content of particular entries ("Tool"). **All of this demonstrates** both the commitment and ability to achieve increasingly higher levels of quality in Wikipedia.

To conclude, Wikipedia, with its breadth, depth, and reliability, serves as an excellent starting point for researchers of virtually any topic. It features millions of entries across a wide range of topics which are updated constantly. Researchers can

confidently turn to it for comprehensive and mostly unbiased information on even the most complex and controversial of topics. While some fear that having too many contributors will lead to inaccurate and even harmful content, measures to ensure that the quality of the entries is maintained have allowed Wikipedia to achieve a level of accuracy close to that of other, more conventional encyclopedias. Though not perfect, Wikipedia has demonstrated that the potential of the internet to decentralize sources of information and empower people can be achieved.

Exercise 4

p. 75

Answers will vary.

(Example answers)

1. <u>It can be argued that</u> language students should train themselves to think as native speakers.

2. <u>There is a great deal of research which indicates that</u> infants have an ability to acquire a limitless number of languages.

3. <u>It can be argued that</u> bilingualism is difficult to achieve without proper instruction.

4. <u>There is little doubt that</u> foreign languages cannot be acquired effectively when learners are not motivated.

5. <u>It seems likely that</u> the speed of language learning increases when learners are given tasks which are slightly above their current level of ability.

Exercise 5

p. 77

1. Therefore, / Accordingly, / Consequently, / In other words,

2. However, / In contrast,

3. Therefore, / Accordingly, / Consequently,

4. For example, / For instance,

5. Therefore, / Accordingly, / Consequently, / As a result,

Exercise 6

p. 79

Answers will vary.

(Example answers)

Early Foreign Language Education

Starting more than three decades ago, learning English has steadily become one of the most common free-time activities for non-native speaking English people of all ages. *For instance, / For example,* busy business people may attend late night classes, or the elderly often attend group lessons as a social activity. Young children have also started to learn English. *In addition, / For instance, / For example,* 30% of parents of preschool-aged children said they had plans to enroll their children in English schools ("Parental"). *In addition, / Moreover, / Furthermore,* some parents are sending their children to middle or high schools overseas an effort to give them a head start on a glamorous international career. *Although* many people believe in the promise of an early English education, starting at too early an age can create problems. Studying English at a young age can lead to low achievement in native as well as foreign language acquisition and also lead to cultural identification difficulties in children . . .

First, / First of all, teaching young children English should require more caution because it can negatively affect their acquisition of both native and foreign languages. *Furthermore, / For instance, / For example,* many researchers suggest that if children are totally immersed in a foreign language before they acquire the basic rules and structures of their mother tongue, it might limit their learning of the foreign language at the advanced level (Saddler 155). *In addition, / Moreover, / Furthermore, / Therefore,* if learners use a foreign language primarily at the critical ages for learning native language, it would hamper their native language development . . .

Proponents of early foreign language education argue that language is most effectively learned when learners are young. *For instance, / For example,* the Critical Period Hypothesis in foreign language acquisition advocates that people learn the sounds of language best before the age of six, or before puberty (Johnson and Newport 70). *However, / In contrast, / On the other hand,* there is a great deal of research which demonstrates that learners who started learning as college students can also acquire the correct sounds of a target language if they are in the proper environment (Wiley 216). *In other words,* early foreign language education is not necessary because it can harm one's acquisition of both native and foreign languages, and the second language can be learned well after the establishment of the first language. *In addition,* teaching young children English can make them feel confused about their cultural identities . . .

UNIT 3 PART 3

> ## Exercise 1

p. 83

The Democratizing of Knowledge: in Defense of Wikipedia

As the internet gained popularity, **many** hoped it would develop as a decentralizing and democratizing force where people could share information and learn from each other. Wikipedia, a free online encyclopedia and the world's largest reference resource, embodies such ideals in allowing multiple users to write and revise content. This collaborative practice differs from the process of compiling conventional encyclopedias, which relies on scholars and experts to contribute information. Wikipedia's

underlying **belief** is that by having more participants contributing and editing information, each entry will have greater range, depth, and accuracy. **Some,** however, claim such thinking is naïve and fundamentally flawed due to the belief that a reliance on amateur editors will lead to inaccurate and unreliable entries. Yet, Wikipedia does provide a useful starting point for research, offering a comprehensive overview of complex topics, a neutral editorial stance, and a dedicated commitment to quality.

Launched in 2001, Wikipedia has become a valuable resource of information in a **relatively** short amount of time. One reason for this quick growth and for its reliability is the collective participation of a vast range of contributors from around the world. The number of people who contribute or edit information on Wikipedia is in the hundreds of thousands (Soneff). Furthermore, these contributions have to be facts that are verifiable, and entries must be unbiased and based on secondary research. Researchers at Dartmouth College concluded that these large numbers and the rules for contribution **indicate** that Wikipedia users are accessing information which is constantly being updated and checked for errors, therefore ensuring the information is accurate, which is a feature not available with traditional encyclopedias. Wikipedia's value is also evident in the breadth of information available. Olivia Solon, news editor at Wired.co.uk states that Wikipedia carries over 3.5 million entries across a diverse variety of topics ranging from the technical to the trivial. Furthermore, Wikipedia features hyperlinks within entries to related topics/terms, providing users with direct access to additional sources which **may** lead to a deeper understanding of a topic. Moreover, Wikipedia is not exclusive to those who can read English: not only is it **one of** the most frequented websites in the world, but it is also a multilingual resource with 270 non-English Wikipedia sites ("User-generated"). The result is a website which is a useful "one-stop" resource for research across disciplines and languages. The success of Wikipedia, therefore, has democratized knowledge through its vast amount of accurate and up-to-date information, and through its **belief** that any responsible user or contributor can access and add knowledge for the benefit of all people.

Together with its vast scope, the principle that all Wikipedia entries should be comprehensive and balanced makes it an especially valuable research tool. Academic research involves grappling with complex issues, concepts, or events, which is precisely what Wikipedia does. For example, the term *globalization* is especially controversial. **For many,** globalization means exploitation and widespread injustice (Scheve and Slaughter 4); for others, globalization is a beneficial force (Wolf 36). This disparity means it is especially important for researchers to comprehensively understand why the term is so controversial. Wikipedia, with its large number of contributors representing a range of **possible** points of view, provides detailed descriptions, the variety of perspectives on the issue, and the reasons for the controversy. Wikipedia's policy also ensures that neutrality is maintained, which is crucial for academic research on issues which are fiercely contested. Globalization issues involve pro-globalization and anti-globalization arguments, but both sides are described comprehensively in the Wikipedia entry on the topic. Indeed, this is only possible because Wikipedia is a free, Web-based resource that presents the breadth and depth of meanings associated with complex, contentious terms in a balanced way. This accessibility to unbiased information **helps** ensure that research results are accurate because the user is able to analyze and carefully consider all sides of an issue.

Despite such benefits, Wikipedia continues to attract critics, who claim there are significant weaknesses with its philosophy of complete openness. One **perceived** weakness is with the contributors, **many** of whom are not scholars or experts on the topics to which they add or alter information. The worry is that Wikipedia, by having entries which anyone can edit, is not a dependable resource because it is filled with incorrect, biased information ("Wikipedia"). Nevertheless, Wikipedia does employ a dedicated team of volunteer administrators whose job it is to quickly remedy inaccurate information. Furthermore, controversial entries can be tagged to indicate when information is under dispute and to encourage users to investigate the dispute and provide more input. Professor of communications Jonathan Thornton maintains that "the service revolves around a set of procedures that are carefully designed to ensure accurate articles through sufficient self-policing and self-amending." A study by the journal *Nature* indeed showed that Wikipedia is **nearly** as accurate as *Britannica* (Giles 900). A further concern is over vandalism of entries with false, malicious information, **often** aiming to hurt the reputation of **certain** people or organizations. However, this matter is being addressed through various measures. For example, software is being developed to swiftly detect words not consistent with the content of **particular** entries ("Tool"). All of this demonstrates both the commitment and ability to achieve increasingly higher levels of quality in Wikipedia.

To conclude, Wikipedia, with its breadth, depth, and reliability, serves as an excellent starting point for researchers of virtually any topic. It features millions of entries across a wide range of topics which are updated constantly. Researchers can confidently turn to it for comprehensive and **mostly** unbiased information on even the most complex and controversial of topics. While **some** fear that having too many contributors will lead to inaccurate and even harmful content, measures to ensure that the quality of the entries is maintained have allowed Wikipedia to achieve a level of accuracy **close to** that of other, more conventional encyclopedias. Though not perfect, Wikipedia has demonstrated that the potential of the internet to decentralize sources of information and empower people can be achieved.

Exercise 2

p. 84

A native English speaker's judgment on the ability of a language learner often depends on pronunciation. ~~Good pronunciation makes a speaker sound fluent in~~ ~~the language~~. Thus, if learners wish to be regarded as fluent, they need to practice pronunciation, not grammar. ~~Focusing on pronunciation helps more than studying structure and words~~. Can a non-native speaker talk like a native English speaker without knowledge of grammar and a large vocabulary? Theoretically it is possible because native speakers do not always talk grammatically and may often use words incorrectly. ~~Native speakers make grammar mistakes and may use a limited vocabulary~~. However, if students wish to achieve an advanced level of English, naturally, they need to have more than good pronunciation. ~~Good pronunciation is not enough to make a non-native speaker an effective user of the language~~.

Exercise 3

p. 85

Answers will vary.

(Example answers; **boldfacing** indicates changed parts, and ~~crossed out~~ items are to be removed)

1. An English learner's native language ~~is the one that~~ influences their learning most.

2. Each language has a set of ~~good~~ phrases to express sympathy and gratitude.

3. Maintaining students' motivation is an important ~~thing~~ *aim* for teachers.

4. At times, language teaching can be ~~a difficult job~~ *stressful and demanding*.

5. Selected texts, if ~~good~~ *interesting and at an appropriate level of difficulty*, can motivate students to read more and increase their reading speed.

Exercise 4

p. 87

Answers will vary; however, the following points require revision:

Introduction

- Tone should be more objectively academic (i.e., remove references to *you* or *they*).
- Off-topic information should be removed (e.g., "Besides, Europe is a wonderful place to visit!").
- In the thesis statement, the three main ideas of each body paragraph need to be stated explicitly.

First Body Paragraph

- The points made on languages being "creations of the human brain" require explanation.
- The sentence ". . . we share our thoughts with other people living in different regions of the world" is also vague and requires clarification.
- The final sentence is redundant (off topic) and should be removed.

Second Body Paragraph
- The sentence "It was found that there are differences between the thought process of trilingual adults and monolingual adults" requires support and explanation (or should be removed).

Third Body Paragraph
- Consists entirely of several seemingly random and unconnected points, and so should be removed.

Fourth Body Paragraph
- The phrase "Some people may disagree" is vague.
- The topic sentence lacks a specific controlling idea.
- The rebuttal ("However, this is not true as I said earlier") needs strengthening (i.e., a main point needs to be stated and support added).
- The final sentence in the paragraph contains too many vague ideas (e.g., "different from each other" or "different parts of the brain").

Conclusion
- There is no re-stated thesis.
- The personal tone and use of *I* is not academic and reduces the significance of the essay's ideas.
- A new, more logical final thought, based on the evidence presented in the essay, should be added.

UNIT 4 PART 1

Exercise 1

p. 91

Answers will vary.

(Example answers)
1. Movies and books
   1) Their entertainment value
   2) How beneficial they are for children's development
2. Team sports and individual sports
   1) Which can be practiced more easily
   2) Which types of people each is suitable for
3. Studying at a university in your own country and studying abroad
   1) The benefits gained from each
   2) Their contributions to one's personality development

Exercise 7

p. 92

Answers will vary.

(Example answers)
1. Movies and books

Reason for comparison 1: Their entertainment value	Reason for comparison 2: How beneficial they are for children's development
Points: a. type of stimulation provided b. location / venue of the activity c. communal vs. solitary activity	Points: a. mental development b. academic skills c. verbal ability

2. Team sports and individual sports

Reason for comparison 1: Which can be practiced more easily	Reason for comparison 2: Which types of people each is suitable for
Points: a. time of practice b. place of practice c. other people needed for practice	Points: a. skills / abilities to learn from each b. shared vs. full responsibility c. source and type of motivation needed to play each

3. Studying at a university in your own country and studying abroad

Reason for comparison 1: The benefits gained from each	Reason for comparison 2: Their contributions to one's personality development
Points: a. Usefulness for future careers b. support from friends and family c. costs	Points: a. to learn independence b. to learn adaptability to unexpected circumstances c. to learn cultural awareness

Exercise 3

p. 94

Answers will vary.

(Example answers)
1. Movies and books (comparison 2)
   Books are more beneficial for children than movies because books enhance children's mental development, academic skills, and verbal ability.

2. Team sports and individual sports (comparison 1)
Because they are usually not tied to a certain place, time, or the presence of other participants, most individual sports can be practiced more easily than team sports.

3. Studying at a university in your own country and studying abroad (comparison 1)
Studying at a university in one's home country and studying abroad are very different in terms of their usefulness for one's future career, the personal support available, and the costs involved.

Exercise 4

p. 96

Sample essay A follows the subject-by-subject pattern.

Sample essay B follows the point-by-point pattern.

Exercise 5

p. 97

Answers will vary.

(Example answers)

1. Movies and books (comparison 2)

Point of comparison	Books	Movies
Mental development	• As readers need to "see" scenes and characters in their minds, books develop and improve imagination. • Books aid concentration as one needs to pay attention constantly to be able to follow the content.	• Movies hamper imagination by depicting every detail explicitly. • Most movies "feed" information to viewers in an easy-to-follow manner, so often less concentration is needed.
Academic skills	• Most books, because of their complexity, encourage and improve higher-level learning and hierarchical thinking, which are necessary academic skills. • Frequent reading is useful in improving one's writing skills.	• Many movies are less complex than books and are often made to entertain rather than stimulate mentally. • Movies have less immediate influence on one's academic or professional performance.
Verbal ability	• Use of higher-level vocabulary is common in most books. • Complex syntax with exposure to compound and complex sentences is common in most books.	• Often lower-level vocabulary is used in movies. • Utterances are less complex syntactically, often not even full sentences but only fragments.

2. Team sports and individual sports (comparison 1)

Point of comparison	Team sports	Individual sports
Time of practice	• Because various people are involved, practice time needs to be arranged beforehand. • As games ideally need to be played out, a certain minimum time exists for most practice activities.	• Can be practiced at any time; can be practiced on a sudden impulse or when time unexpectedly becomes available. • Can be practiced for any length of time.
Place of practice	• Normally tied to a specific place, such as a court or gymnasium. • Harder to arrange when the venue needs to be changed, such as while traveling or in case of unavailability of or damage to original practice venue.	• Can normally be practiced with fewer or no place restrictions. • Easier to adapt to areas or locations different from one's normal practice location.
Other people needed for practice	• A certain minimum number of people are often needed for team practice. • Specific, irreplaceable people are often needed for serious team practice when preparing for games or tournaments.	• Can normally be enjoyed alone or with a flexible number of other people. • It is normally easy to practice with different / various partners.

3. Studying at a university in your own country and studying abroad (comparison 1)

Point of comparison	Studying at a university in own country	Studying abroad
Usefulness for future careers	• Students could make use of great career opportunities and connections that can come up during regular studies in one's home country. • By staying in the education system of the same country, students may be able to study the field they are interested in more consistently and without interruptions.	• Experience of any type abroad is often seen as a plus by prospective employers. • Students could encounter and internalize various useful skills and abilities which are hard or impossible to gain in one's home country.
Support from friends and family	• Students can enjoy support from their families. • Most college-age people have many friends to rely on in their home countries.	• Most students will have no family in the foreign target country. • Fewer, if any, friends will exist abroad.
Costs	• Tuition is normally cheaper. • Living expenses are normally cheaper, and living with parents is often possible.	• Tuition may be much more expensive. • Living expenses are often much higher.

UNIT 4 PART 2

Exercise 1

p. 103

1. **Similarities:**

    also, likewise, similarly, both . . . and . . . , not only
    . . . but also . . . , neither . . . nor . . . , as, just as . . .
    so too, as . . . as, like, alike, similar to, same as

    Differences:

    however, in contrast, instead, nevertheless,
    nonetheless, still, on the contrary, but, yet,
    although, even though, whereas, while, despite,
    in spite of, be dissimilar, unlike, differ in/from, at
    the same time

2.

Sample essay A:

Educating Students in Public and Home Schools

One of the top concerns of parents is their children's
education. **Yet**, how and where they can receive the
best quality education remains open to debate. In
the United States, traditional public schools remain
the common choice for most parents, **but** a growing
number are choosing to school their children in their
own homes. Officially, **both** school options must
follow the **same** educational guidelines established
by their respective state. Having these guidelines
suggests that students study in **similar** ways in each
school environment. **However**, the guidelines only
set goals for students, so the methods each form
of education adopts to reach these goals can vary
considerably. How students are educated in public
schools and home schools is quite **different** in terms
of the curriculum, quality of teaching, and in the
interaction with other students.

When looking at public schools, aspects of their
educational environments are determined by
the fact that they are public institutions with a
diversity of students. One of these aspects is the
curriculum. **Along with** core courses in language,
math, and science, broad-ranging courses such as
history, geography, music, physical education, and
social studies are offered in order to provide a
comprehensive education (Bielick 4). This variety in
courses serves to expose students to a wide range of
subjects, thereby giving them a chance to discover
which subjects might be of particular interest.
Moreover, public schools must monitor and report
to education officials on the effectiveness of the
curriculum (Ravitch 10). This ensures that the quality
of the curriculum is maintained and that goals are
reached. **Additionally,** the teachers themselves are
crucial in public education. American College Testing
(ACT) argues that along with their specialized course
knowledge and educational training, the variety
in teachers' styles and personalities can stimulate
students and foster a deeper appreciation for subjects
in **both** interested students, and in students who may
not even enjoy the subject ("Benefits" 2). Considering
the number of courses offered during the years of
school education, changing teachers regularly can be

an enriching experience for students. A third critical
aspect in public school education is the students
themselves. Romanowski points out that public school
students routinely exchange ideas and work together
in groups. **While** they may not always like each other,
they learn to adapt and cope with the diversity of
backgrounds, values, and experience present among
students in a public school class (82). This facilitates
a type of learning beyond what books or even a
teacher can provide, but which forms an essential
element in learning to live in a diverse society. In
short, diversity seems to be a major asset found in the
public school educational environment.

Home schools, **however**, offer a **contrasting**
education environment to public schools due to the
more private nature of their learning environment.
The curriculum in home schools, for instance, is
much more flexible **than** in public schools. **Despite**
having to officially teach the **same** curriculum as
public schools, most states in the U.S. have **fewer**
regulations for home schools ("Homeschooling
Thru"). This lack of regulation led to a *New York
Times* report that found the majority of home
schools do not submit any information to local school
officials (*Homeschooling Regulations*). **While** some
critics may argue that it is **more** likely for students in
home schools to be deprived of a diverse education,
many home school advocates believe that a **less**
regulated curriculum allows it to be shaped according
to the interests and skill level of individual students,
thereby making it **more** educationally beneficial to
the student. Furthermore, as the curriculum at home
schools is **less** regulated **than** in public schools, **so too**
are teachers at home schools. Home school teachers
require no special teacher training or expertise in
all of the subjects taught, which leads to criticism
over the qualification of these teachers to actually
teach (Romanowski 80). **However**, it can be argued
that the personal attention a student in a home
school receives leads to better academic performance
than can be achieved with a certified teacher
teaching a class with a large number of students.
Lastly, perhaps one of the most significant **contrasts**
between public and home schools is the society of
other students. **While** home school students can
interact with each other via the internet and even
participate in occasional field trips, they generally
spend their day alone with a parent, or in some cases,
a small group ("Homeschooling Thru"). **Although**
this prevents them from experiencing the diversity
to be found in public schools, it is a situation some
parents prefer. In her report for the National Center
for Education Statistics, for example, Bielick found
that almost 75% of parents chose to home-school
their children for religious or moral reasons (2). This
suggests that home-schooled students are purposely
kept apart from others to ensure only family beliefs
are taught, or even to prevent them from being
negatively influenced by classmates. In all, therefore,
homeschooling has become an option for those
who relate quality of education with flexibility and
personal attention – aspects which give teachers,
often a parent, **more** control in shaping the learning
experience of their student.

In conclusion, public and home schools have
contrasting attributes which result in **different**

educational styles and benefits. In public schools, **more** regulated learning and more diversity in the curriculum, teachers, and students can be expected. Many people see this as important in preparing students for later life. Home schools, on the **other hand**, are **less** regulated and thereby offer parents the opportunity to exercise **greater** control over what their children are learning and with whom they are socializing. These considerable **differences** between public and home schools mean that parents will have to assess their own definition of quality education if they are considering either option for their children.

Sample essay B:

Educating Students in Public and Home Schools

One of the top concerns of parents is their children's education. **Yet,** how and where they can receive the best quality education remains open to debate. In the United States, traditional public schools remain the common choice for most parents, but a growing number are choosing to school their children in their own homes. Officially, **both** school options must follow the **same** educational guidelines established by their respective state. Having these guidelines suggests that students study in similar ways in each school environment. **However**, the guidelines only set goals for students, so the methods each form of education adopts to reach these goals can vary considerably. How students are educated in public schools and home schools is quite **different** in terms of the curriculum, quality of teaching, and in the interaction with other students.

One of the major **differences** between public and home schools affecting how students are educated is the curriculum. Public school curriculums are designed around serving a diverse range of students with diverse interests. **Along with** core courses in language, math, and science, broad-ranging courses such as history, geography, music, physical education, and social studies are offered in order to provide a comprehensive education (Bielick 4). This variety in courses serves to expose students to a wide range of subjects, thereby giving them a chance to discover which subjects might be of particular interest. Moreover, public schools must monitor and report to education officials on the effectiveness of the curriculum (Ravitch 10). This ensures that the quality of the curriculum is maintained and that goals are reached. The curriculum in home schools, **however**, is much **more** flexible **than** in public schools. **Despite** having to officially teach the **same** curriculum as public schools, most states in the U.S. have **fewer** regulations for home schools ("Homeschooling Thru"). This lack of regulation led to a *New York Times* report that found the majority of home schools do not submit any information to local school officials (*Homeschooling Regulations*). **While** some critics may argue that it is **more** likely for students in home schools to be deprived of a diverse education, many home school advocates believe that a **less** regulated curriculum allows it to be shaped according to the interests and skill level of individual students, thereby making it **more** educationally beneficial to the student. Therefore, parents considering the best type of education for their children need to consider whether a curriculum's diversity or flexibility should be given priority.

While the curriculum is important, the teachers of the curriculum are **also** a key factor in determining how students learn. In public schools, having teachers who are **not only** certified **but** specialized in particular subjects is seen as an asset. American College Testing (ACT) argues that along with their specialized course knowledge and educational training, the variety in teachers' styles and personalities can stimulate students and foster a **deeper** appreciation for subjects in **both** interested students and in students who may not even enjoy the subject ("Benefits" 2). Considering the number of courses offered during the years of school education, changing teachers regularly can be an enriching experience for students in public schools. Most home school teachers, **however**, are the only teacher for a particular student, and often this teacher is the student's parent and not certified as a teacher. Home school teachers require no special teacher training or expertise in all of the subjects taught, which leads to criticism over the qualification of these teachers to actually teach (Romanowski 80). **However,** it can be argued that the personal attention a student in a home school receives leads to **better** academic performance **than** can be achieved by a certified teacher teaching a class with a large number of students. Assessing the teaching situation in public and home schools, then, is another crucial consideration for parents seeking the ideal learning opportunity for their children.

A third critical aspect **differentiating** the education in public and home schools is the presence of other students. In public schools, student populations are often large and diverse, which some see as a major asset. Romanowski points out that public school students routinely exchange ideas and work together in groups. **While** they may not always like each other, they learn to adapt and cope with the diversity of backgrounds, values, and experience present among students in a public school class (82). This facilitates a type of learning beyond what books or even a teacher can provide, **but** which forms an essential element in learning to live in a diverse society. **On the other hand**, students in home schools are in a very **different** situation. **While** home school students can interact with each other via the internet and even participate in occasional field trips, they generally spend their day alone with a parent, or in some cases, a small group. ("Homeschooling Thru"). **Although** this prevents them from experiencing the diversity to be found in public schools, it is a situation some parents prefer. In her report for the National Center for Education Statistics, Bielick found that almost 75% of parents chose to home-school their children for religious or moral reasons (2). This suggests that home-schooled students are purposely kept apart from others to ensure only family beliefs are taught, or even to prevent them from being negatively influenced by classmates. Therefore, when weighing quality of education in public versus home schools, parents must decide whether the presence of other students is a benefit or drawback.

In conclusion, public and home schools have **contrasting** attributes which result in **different** educational styles and benefits. In public schools, **more** regulated learning and more diversity in the curriculum, teachers, and students can be expected. Many people see this as important in preparing students for later life. Home schools, **on the other hand**, are **less** regulated and thereby offer parents the opportunity to exercise **greater** control over what their children are learning and with whom they are socializing. These considerable **differences** between public and home schools mean that parents will have to assess their own definition of quality education if they are considering either option for their children.

Exercise 2

p. 105

1. both
2. similar to
3. Also
4. Neither
5. similarly
6. Like

Exercise 3

p. 107

1. Unlike
2. However / In contrast
3. but / whereas
4. however
5. However / In contrast
6. Compared to

Exercise 4

p. 108

1. ✗

   The phrase *sometimes school property is damaged* could be changed to *damage to school property*.

2. ✗

   The phrase *they have lower motivation levels* could be changed to *how motivated they are*.

3. ✓
4. ✗

   The phrase *and students have many chances to learn at their own pace* could be changed to *more chances to learn at their own pace*.

5. ✓
6. ✗

   They should be removed from the second clause.

UNIT 4 PART 3

Exercise 1

p. 110

1. Unlike girls, <u>boys</u> find diagrams easier to understand than wordy explanations.
2. <u>Boys who study in single-sex classes</u> often achieve better results than boys in mixed classes.
3. When listening, <u>boys</u> often do not hear as many details as girls.

4. After the lunchtime break, <u>both boys and girls</u> often have trouble concentrating in class.
5. While girls often want to be regarded as good students, <u>boys</u> are usually less keen to please adults.
6. <u>Girls</u> hear better in class than boys, and teachers in all-girl classes are less likely to shout to control their students.

Exercise 2

p. 111

1. **Recommendation; a** is more effective while recommendation **b** is too simplistic ("students who wish to live abroad should choose to study overseas")
2. **Opinion; b** is more effective while **a** is overly subjective and unsupported (e.g., "by far the best option")
3. **Prediction; b** is more effective while **a** does not seem logical (why would a "globalized" society make it "difficult for students to decide"?)
4. **Solution; a** is more effective while **b** is overly simplified ("both systems offer advantages," "both have significant bad points")

Exercise 3

p. 114

Whole essay

1. Yes.
2. It follows the subject-by-subject style (five paragraphs).

Introductory paragraph

3. The first sentence is an acceptable hook, although it probably does not raise enough interest for some readers. The hook idea continues for the next four sentences, which do raise interest effectively, but as the use of questions is generally not appropriate in academic essays, these parts should be rewritten as statements.
4. Yes, but see 3 above.
5. Yes, although "perform differently" alone in the last main idea may not be clear enough. Perhaps "academically" could be added.
6. Yes.
7. **TS1** could have a clearer controlling idea.
   TS2 does not state the topic.
   TS3 is built on cited information that is unacceptable in a topic sentence, which should always be worded by the writer of the essay.
8. Yes / Yes.
9. N/A
10. **Body 1**
    - the claim that boys "use fewer words than girls and prefer to work silently on tasks" needs to be supported by evidence.

- The final sentence also contains an argument that would be stronger cited.
- There is no concluding sentence.

Body 2

- Mostly a logical flow of ideas, but most claims are unsubstantiated. As only one type 2 sentence is used, and that is in the wrong place (the last sentence should never be a type 2 sentence), it cannot be said that the waltz is followed.
- The final transition (*but*) is inappropriate, which also influences the smooth flow of ideas.
- There is no concluding sentence.

Body 3

- Starting with a type 2 sentence is unacceptable.
- The second sentence starting with "Everyone knows" is an unsubstantiated overgeneralization.
- "Of course" is an inappropriate and illogical transition.
- The concluding sentence should be more detailed.

11. Yes

Concluding paragraph

12. Yes.

13. Yes.

14. There is a final thought, but its first clause is repetitive and its second sounds like a truism without specifying who should consider these differences and why.

15. Yes.

Language/coherence

16. Yes.

17. Yes.

18. There is a parallel structure error in the last main idea of the thesis. Another error is in the second sentence of Body 2 ("neither following rules nor respect the teacher").

Exercise 4

p. 115

Comments are always listed in order of their appearance in the essays.

Q #	Essay A	Essay B
1a.	*Girls tend to get better results in high school and at university because formal education favors girls' natural behavior, teaching styles in most schools are more suited to girls than boys, and girls tend to be more motivated than boys.*	*Girls tend to get better results in high school because formal education favors girls' natural behavior, teaching styles in most schools are more suited to girls than boys, and girls tend to be more motivated than boys.*
1b.	Yes.	Yes.
2a.	**TS1:** *Formal education does not favor boys' natural behavior.* **TS2:** *The second reason for girls' success compared to boys is that the teaching style often favors girls.* **TS3:** *It has been pointed out that girls are more motivated and conscientious than boys.*	**TS1:** *The first reason that girls fare better in school is that the school system tends to favor girls' natural behavior.* **TS2:** *Another reason for girls' success compared to boys is that teaching styles often favor girls.* **TS2:** *A further reason why girls perform better at school than boys is because they are generally more motivated than boys.*
2b.	**TS1** lacks controlling idea. **TS2** should explain which institution the paragraph is going to focus on (i.e., high school?) more clearly. **TS3** lacks controlling idea, and the wording at the beginning ("It has been pointed out") may give the wrong impression to the reader, namely that this is not the writers idea but someone else's (i.e., a counter-argument).	Yes.
3a.	**Body 1:** - *Boys are more likely to feel "anti-education"* - *boys are encouraged to play sports and be loud outside school* - *girls are expected to talk* **Body 2:** - *girls adopt feminine teaching styles better than boys do* **Body 3:** - *girls are more motivated and conscientious than boys* - *girls put more effort into their work and spend more time doing homework properly.*	**Body 1:** - *Whereas girls have this culture [of being quiet, accepting authority, and following rules] imposed on them when they are young, boys do not.* - *[Boys] are often encouraged to play sports, be loud, and be aggressive.* - *girls are raised to be fit for school education while boys are not* - *Boys are expected to learn how to adopt school culture through the eternal conflicts with school authorities.* **Body 2:** - *Another reason for girls' success compared to boys is that teaching styles often favor girls.*

		- "boys' performance has been made worse by the feminine influences of female teachers and the very nature of the English curriculum itself" - boys "frequently dominate the classroom environment and do not listen to female teachers" - feminine teaching styles in most schools contribute to girls' superior academic performance **Body 3:** - [girls] are generally more motivated than boys - girls are more motivated and conscientious than boys - [girls] put more effort into their work and spend more time doing homework properly, and they take care in how their work is presented - boys do not seem well motivated to submit homework on time
3b.	Yes, but Body 3 needs to be developed more.	Yes.
4.	Subject by subject	Subject by subject
5a.	- Douglas stated that "school is essentially a linguistic experience and most subjects require good levels of comprehension and writing skills" (45). - Martino and Meyenne said that "gender-conflict is brought to the attention of public schools in various forms" (303).	- Douglas stated that "girls are raised to be fit for school education while boys are not. Boys are expected to learn how to adopt school culture through the eternal conflicts with school authorities" (199). - Martino and Meyenne (303) said that "boys' performance has been made worse by the feminine influences of female teachers and the very nature of the English curriculum itself."

		- Warrington and Younger also wrote that boys "frequently dominate the classroom environment and do not listen to female teachers" (2000). - Mikos and Brown (180) pointed out that girls are more motivated and conscientious than boys. - In contrast, boys do not seem well motivated to submit homework on time (qtd. in Otani 230).
5b.	Yes	Yes, but in several cases the citations are left uninterpreted or unexplained, which is contrary to what students have learned about paragraph waltz.
6a.	- . . . (get) better (results) . . . - . . . more (suited to girls) than . . . - . . . (tend to be) more (motivated) . . . - . . . more (likely to feel) . . . - . . . (success) compared to (boys is) . . . - . . . (teaching styles) better than (boys do) . . . - . . . (girls are) more (motivated and conscientious) than (boys) - . . . (put) more (effort into . . .) - . . . (tend to get) better (academic results) . . .	- . . . (get) better (results) . . . - . . . more (suited to girls) than . . . - . . . (tend to be) more (motivated) . . . - . . . (fare) better (at school) . . . - Whereas (girls have) . . . - . . . (education) while (boys) . . . - . . . (success) compared to (boys) . . . - . . . (perform) better (at school) . . . - . . . (girls are) more (motivated and conscientious) than (boys) - . . . (spend) more (time) . . . - In contrast (, boys) . . .
6b.	Yes.	Yes.
7a.	- On the other hand - In this way - (The) second (reason) - Therefore - In conclusion	- (The) first (reason) - Instead - Another (reason) - (Warrington and Younger) also (wrote that) - In this way - (A) further (reason) - In conclusion

	Column A	Column B
7b.	Yes, although the use of *therefore* in the last sentences of body 2 is perhaps a little too large leap of logic.	Yes.
8.	**Introductory paragraph** - Hook and building sentences are missing. **Body 1** - TS1 lacks controlling idea. - Use of you in Body 1 should be avoided. **Body 2** - TS2 should explain which institution the sentence is focusing on (e.g., high school) more clearly. - The Martino and Meyenne citation should be linked more logically, and a better reporting verb should be used instead of said. - *Therefore* at the end of Body 2 could be replaced with a more suitable transition. **Body 3** - TS3 lacks controlling idea, and the wording at the beginning ("It has been pointed out") may give the wrong impression to the reader, namely that this is not the writer's idea but someone else's (i.e., a counter-argument). - The paragraph needs to be more developed overall with at least one citation added. - The concluding sentence is missing. **Concluding paragraph** - The concluding paragraph is underdeveloped. - The restated thesis and main ideas are missing. - The recommendation in the final thought is simplistic and unrealistic. **Overall** - More varied phrases for comparing and contrasting should be used. The essay relies heavily on simply using comparative forms of adjectives for comparisons. - Transitions could be improved. - More citations are needed to make the arguments stronger.	**Introductory paragraph** - Hook and building sentences are missing. **Body 1** - The final citation is left uncommented upon. - No concluding sentence. **Body 2** - The Martino and Meyenne citation should have a better reporting verb instead of said. Similarly, wrote in the Warrington and Younger source, although acceptable, could also be improved. - The Warrington and Younger source looks like it is cited with year of publication instead of a page number which is APA style and not MLA (although a 2,000+ page book is possible). **Body 3** - The Mikos and Brown citation seems to just repeat the idea in the topic sentence instead of developing it further. Either the topic sentence or the following sentence should be rewritten to avoid this problem. - The final citation claims to be a quoted one, but no quotation marks are used. - The final citation is not interpreted or commented on. - The concluding sentence is missing. **Concluding paragraph** - The final thought is missing. **Overall** The incorrect use of the waltz and lack of type 3 sentences seem to be the main problem.

Appendix A
Choosing active or passive sentences

p. 119

1. a
2. a
3. b
4. a
5. a

Appendix B
Using conjunctive adverbs

Practice exercise 1

p. 121

a. Many people associate bananas with South America. **(However,)** India **(, however,)** is actually the country that produces the most bananas **(, however)**.

b. Most bananas grown in India are consumed domestically. **(Therefore,)** India **(, therefore,)** is not well known as an exporter of bananas **(, therefore)**.

c. Bananas are a good source of energy, vitamin B6, and potassium. **(As a result,)** Many athletes eat them **(as a result,)** as part of a nutritionally balanced diet **(as a result)**.

d. The bananas that you see in the supermarket are usually yellow with brown spots which show that they are ready to be eaten. **(In fact,)** Thanks to technology, **(in fact,)** bananas can **(in fact)** be harvested up to one month earlier and are transported in special refrigerated containers to prevent ripening.

e. In Europe and North America, ripe bananas are eaten as fruit or used in deserts. **(On the other hand,)** In many tropical countries, **(on the other hand,)** bananas are eaten green and cooked like potatoes **(on the other hand)**.

Practice exercise 2

p. 121

Many South American countries are banana exporters. The most common variety of banana found in supermarkets today is the Dwarf Cavendish. **In comparison,** until the 1950s, another variety, Gros Michel, was the most popular around the world. It was almost completely wiped out by a leaf disease, **however**. The Cavendish banana is resilient against the disease, and **thus** became the most commonly grown. Cavendish bananas are all genetically identical. **As a result**, scientists think there is a realistic possibility that they too could be susceptible to disease and be wiped out in the future. Efforts are, **therefore**, being undertaken in Honduras to develop new, disease resilient varieties of banana.

Appendix C
Using acronyms and initialisms

Practice exercise

p. 122

(**Boldfacing** indicates added or changed parts, and ~~crossed out~~ items are to be removed.)

After World War II, Spain has played a role in numerous influential international organizations in economic, military, and sporting areas. It became part of the United Nations **(UN)** in 1955, when member countries saw it as a valuable ally in the Cold War. Spain now contributes to international UN aid efforts, such as making grants to developing countries in order to encourage climate change measures, and is one of the top five ~~United Nations~~ **(UN)** contributors in aid for human rights. After becoming a democracy, Spain joined the North Atlantic Treaty Organization **(NATO)** in 1982, and was seen as a valuable ally due to its important strategic position next to the Mediterranean Sea and the Strait of Gibraltar. Spanish forces contributed to NATO operations in both Iraq and Afghanistan. Finally, there is the contribution to the International Olympics Committee ~~(IOC)~~. The second longest serving president of this organization was a Spaniard named Juan Antonio Samaranch, who served from 1980 to 2001.

Appendix D
Placing adverbs of frequency

Practice exercise 1

p. 124

a. always
b. rarely, never, hardly ever, seldom
c. often, occasionally, frequently, usually, sometimes

Practice exercise 2

p. 124

(**Boldfacing** indicates added or changed parts, and ~~crossed out~~ items are to be removed.)

a. ✗ Although bears in the wild will sometimes approach humans, they **usually** try to avoid people ~~usually~~.

b. ✓

c. ✗ ~~Never, are people~~ **Never are people / People are never** legally permitted to operate an automobile without first obtaining a driver's license.

d. ✗ Grits, a common breakfast delicacy in the southeastern United States, are hardly **ever** found in restaurants in northern states ~~ever~~.

e. ✗ Failing to pay attention to the road ~~often is~~ **is often** a factor in traffic accidents.

Practice exercise 3

p. 124

a. Although there are exceptions, professional athletes **seldom** go through their entire career without sustaining an injury.

b. The most diverse ecosystems have **always** been found in tropical rain forests.

c. Taking short breaks **occasionally** during the workday has been shown by some studies to boost productivity.

d. **Often** able to elude researchers, the giant squid is an animal still shrouded in mystery.

Appendix E
Using quantifiers

Practice exercise 1

p. 126

a. **Many** of the people attending the conference had traveled from countries outside the United States.

b. **Many** animals have been endangered due to human development and migration.

c. Almost all of the students who were asked were unwilling to take part in the experiment, but **a few** of them agreed to participate.

d. Underfunded schools are at a disadvantage because **few** of their textbooks are the most current.

e. Even though they signed the free trade agreement, each country still **has** some taxes on imports.

f. The company secured several important contracts last year, so they gave large bonuses to some of **the** employees.

Practice exercise 2

p. 126

a. According to the study, although **most** of the members taking the drug reported a reduction in symptoms, **many** of those taking the placebo also reported feeling better. Therefore, **more** research is needed before the drug's effect can be fully understood. However, because **a great deal of** money and time are required, and because there is **little** public funding for experimental psychiatric medicines, further experiments are not planned for the near future.

b. After viewing the film, 60 percent of audiences said that they thought the film had too **much** violence. However, despite the fact that they thought it had **some** content which might be inappropriate for minors, **most** viewers said they would consider allowing their children to see the film due to its overall moral message.

c. Although **a number of** people say they wish to climb Mt. Everest at some point in their lives, relatively **few** people actually achieve their goal. One reason **most of** those who wish to go decide not to is because of the **many** dangers involved.

Appendix F
Using punctuation

Practice exercise

p. 129

While rising sea levels will cause major problems for developed countries in the long term, it is developing countries with large areas of low-lying coastal land such as **B**angladesh, **V**ietnam, and **E**gypt which face the more immediate threat. **F**irstly, the increased sea levels will lead to a reduction in the space which is available for living. **F**or example, it has been noted that 27% of **B**angladesh's habitable land will be lost by 2100 as a result of the rise in sea levels. **T**his will lead to a much higher level of population density. **S**econdly, as a result of the rising sea levels, large areas of the countries' agricultural land, which is often located in the coastal regions, will become unusable. **F**or instance, **L**eatherman estimates that 16% of **E**gypt's agricultural land could be lost by 2100. **C**onsequently, these countries will find it difficult to provide enough food to support their populations. **I**t is clear that rapid action needs to be taken in order to protect these developing countries from the devastating effects of rising sea levels**.**

Appendix G
Using negating prefixes

Practice exercise

p. 131

1. It is not possible to add a negative prefix to *dangerous*.

2. *not literate → illiterate*

3. *not being reliable → being unreliable*

4. It is not possible to change *credible*, as *incredible* would change the meaning.

5. *are not interested → are uninterested*

6. *were not represented correctly → were represented incorrectly*

7. *not understood → misunderstood*

8. It is not possible to change *different*, as *indifferent* would change the meaning.